A YEAR

without

MEN

A YEAR

without

MEN

A TWELVE-POINT GUIDE TO

Inspire & Empower Women

ALLISON CARMEN

AUTHOR OF *THE GIFT OF MAYBE*

Skyhorse Publishing

Skyhorse Publishing books may be purchased in bulk at special discounts for sales promotion, corporate gifts, fund-raising, or educational purposes. Special editions can also be created to specifications. For details, contact the Special Sales Department, Skyhorse Publishing, 307 West 36th Street, 11th Floor, New York, NY 10018 or info@skyhorsepublishing.com.

Skyhorse® and Skyhorse Publishing® are registered trademarks of Skyhorse Publishing, Inc.®, a Delaware corporation.

Visit our website at www.skyhorsepublishing.com.

10 9 8 7 6 5 4 3 2 1

Library of Congress Cataloging-in-Publication Data is available on file.

Jacket design by Daniel Brount
Jacket illustrations by Shutterstock and Getty Images

Print ISBN: 978-1-5107-6412-5
Ebook ISBN: 978-1-5107-6413-2

Printed in the United States of America

To my children, Morgan and Amanda.
May my journey inspire you to embrace your truth.
May my journey inspire you to love and value everything that you are.
May my journey inspire you to embrace your strong, independent
spirits as women.

Contents

Introduction xi

Chapter 1: July—Make Friends with Uncertainty 1

Chapter 2: August—Accept That You Can't Stop the Rain 17

Chapter 3: September—Just Because Someone Says It,
Doesn't Make It True 31

Chapter 4: October—Believe in Your Own Beauty 41

Chapter 5: November—There Is Only One Person
You Need to Trust 55

Chapter 6: December and January—Everyone Suffers:
Don't Let It Stop You 63

Chapter 7: February—Respond—Don't React:
You Are *Not* Too Emotional 79

Chapter 8: March—Don't Compare Yourself to Anyone Else 95

Chapter 9: April—Maybe There Is Nothing Wrong with You 109

Chapter 10: May—Let Go and Let Life In 123

Chapter 11: June—Only Expect the Unexpected 133

Chapter 12: Build the House You Want to Live In 143

Acknowledgments 149

A YEAR

without

MEN

Introduction

"Try not to resist the changes that come your way. Instead, let life live through you. And do not worry that your life is turning upside down. How do you know that the side you are used to is better than the one to come?"

—Rumi

* * *

A year ago, I thought I was in a happy and committed marriage. I'd been married to my husband for twenty-seven years, and we'd been together for twenty-nine. Life was full. I had published a self-help book a few years earlier, *The Gift of Maybe: Finding Hope and Possibilities in Uncertain Times*, and I ran a successful, one-woman company as a business consultant and business/life coach with a wide variety of clients. I imagined that as our children got older—they were fifteen and nineteen—I would focus more on the self-help part of my business. I wanted to guide people through difficult and uncertain times, sharing the tools I had gathered in my own journey from a tax lawyer to a businesswoman, as well as a parent. I had struggled a lot in my life physically and emotionally, but I was at a good point in my journey. Most of all, I had my family—two wonderful girls who were blossoming and a husband I loved and was committed to with all my heart.

On June 30, 2018, my husband came home to our New York City apartment where we had lived most of our children's lives and which was filled with so many incredible memories and milestones. He had just returned home from the gym, and I was eating lunch at the kitchen counter. He sat down with his own food a few feet away at the kitchen table and said he wanted to speak to me. I swiveled around on the stool I was on and looked at him, expecting him to bring up our summer vacation plans or our oldest daughter's upcoming year at college. Instead, he blurted out, "I am attracted to other women at the gym, and we need to separate because I want to have sex with other women. We can still have family holidays and family vacations together."

I stared at him, trying to understand. "You are joking with me, right?" I responded. I could think of no other explanation for what he was saying.

We had just celebrated our birthdays with loving poems in May and sent both of our children off to summer programs. A few months earlier, he had launched his new business with my unwavering support. He was my best friend in the world. I searched his face. He looked down.

I repeated, "You are joking, right?"

Without looking up, he said, "I am serious. We need to separate." He continued talking about women at the gym, going into detail about the types of women he was attracted to and his desire to have sex with other women. I stopped hearing his words. I just fell to the floor, hoping to grab something I knew. As I lay there, I wanted to find something to hold me. I remember looking across the room at the wall thinking, *If I could get there and bang my head against that wall, it would hurt less than how I feel right now.* I heard my husband telling me to get up, but he never moved from his seat. I looked up at him, and his eyes appeared glazed over. He had detached from the only world I knew.

What I had imagined would be a fun few weeks of regrouping and sharing special one-on-one time together was turning into the most traumatic time of my life. My entire world had just blown apart. What did he mean, "to separate"? We were married. We were partners in every part of our lives. We had kids together. This was like someone telling me they were going to rip off both of my arms. Shocked, I finally spoke. I begged and begged for him not to leave.

He agreed to go for counseling for three months. My husband and I had gone to marriage counseling a few years earlier for just three sessions to work out some issues. After these sessions, he never said another word about any problems and life seemed good.

This time, although he had committed to three months of counseling, we would not even make it past seven weeks. On August 24, our wedding anniversary, I would leave for the weekend with the girls to my sister's house on Long Island, and he would move out of our family home.

As I entered my sister's guest room that day, I remember taking off my wedding ring and once again falling to the floor. I didn't understand what was happening, I didn't understand how I would exist without this marriage, and I didn't understand what would become of my family. Also, I didn't realize that June 30, 2018, the day he made his announcement, the day he truly left me, would mark the beginning of a yearlong experience in which my daily life was practically devoid of men. This was to be a year without men.

My husband left me. But that alone was not enough to shift my entire perspective about myself as a woman in the world. It was being surrounded by women and in very little contact with men for twelve months that would shift the way I think, act, and feel in business and in my personal life in ways I could never have imagined.

In truth, my life had already begun moving in this man-free direction without my realizing it. In May 2018, I left the Board of Directors of my building, comprised mostly of men, because I had joined the Board of Directors of Girls Educational and Mentoring Services (GEMS). GEMS is a New York City nonprofit organization that empowers girls and young women who have been commercially sexually exploited and domestically trafficked. The organization was women-led, and many women who worked there were survivors themselves.

By the second half of the year, not by my own design, I was no longer working directly with any male clients, apart from my main client with whom I had consulted for twenty-five years. Within a few days of my husband announcing he wanted to separate, my main client stopped communicating with me about his business. He was selling his company and gave the responsibility of managing the sale to his internal management team. He quickly moved away from dealing with many aspects of the business. This break was a natural progression of the sale but was, for me, abrupt and upsetting. I did work at the company with his internal management team for a short time after, but the company was sold in early fall, and my contract was terminated.

While my husband and I were in marriage counseling over the summer, one of my newer clients, The Motherhood Center, asked me to take a more significant role in the company as their part-time chief financial officer. The Motherhood Center is a mission-driven for-profit business that functions as a day hospital for women with perinatal mood and anxiety disorders. The owner, Dr. Catherine Birndorf, a leading psychiatrist in reproductive psychiatry and women's mental health, was in the process of separating from her business partner. Her business partner was the only male at the company. Since the age of twenty-eight, I had been working on my own, and this was a position I might not have considered had my husband not expressed his desire to leave me. Now, it just seemed like a smart move for me, so I committed to fifteen hours a week. I was functioning at my lowest level, and I would drag myself to the Center once or twice a week.

Over the previous few years, I had become close friends with Dr. Birndorf. During this summer, we held meetings with her employees and outside consultants, and in between the meetings I would turn to her and say, "I feel like I am going to die."

She would assure me, "You are not going to die." Then, until the next meeting started, we would talk about my pain. As soon as the next meeting ended, I would turn to her and we did it all over again.

Now, looking back, I think how wise the universe was to put me in that place with Dr. Birndorf—of all therapists and all women—to support me. It was a place where nobody knew my husband other than Dr. Birndorf. The atmosphere was compassionate and empathetic and busy and needy. When you got off the elevator, the hallway was filled with patients' baby carriages, and as you walked into the office you were always greeted like you belonged. The decor was soft and pink, but the place was filled with female warriors saving mothers' lives each day from suicide, depression, and other mental ailments. It was much warmer than any other atmosphere in which I have ever worked. Most of all, it was a place fulfilling a critical mission, and fulfilling it with a strategy of equality, kindness, and understanding.

At the time, I was also working with a healer named Maria Soledad, who was helping me explore my spiritual growth. My own spiritual growth and expansion were always front and center in my life, so I have often engaged with people who do energy work, acupuncture, or integrative medicine. I had been part of the well-being movement for over twenty-five years, long before kale was in every household and everyone practiced yoga. I'd supported the movement as an attorney, business consultant, business coach, and healthy school-food advocate. I infused spirituality and self-help with every business client I had. I prided myself on being aware and conscious, which now makes me laugh. How could someone who helped so many people and businesses, someone with my intelligence and intuition, not see what was happening in her own marriage?

Before my husband actually left at the end of August, while we were still in counseling, Maria, the healer, took my hand one day and said, "He is going to leave you. Your new life journey is about to begin."

I started to scream at her, "Stop saying this! You are wrong! This can't be!" But she was right. He did leave, and I was left on my own to face the world, to face my daughters, my remaining clients, friends, colleagues, and most of all, myself.

So, by the end of August 2018, my husband had moved out, and all of my male clients were gone. My volunteer activities no longer put me in contact with men, and I worked part-time at an all-women company. It wasn't until September 2018 when I looked around and noticed that I was inhabiting a world without men.

My world with next to no contact with men was not a conscious choice. In fact, it actually took me a few months of working at The Motherhood Center before I realized the impact of having no men in my work environment. The dynamic between those of us who worked in the office was different. There were no men bonding over sports or talking about girls. The way everyone expressed themselves was different, so the office atmosphere had a quality I'd never experienced in any workplace before. The conversations were sometimes longer, but nobody seemed to care. Sometimes there were hugs and compliments on each other's shoes. The quality of the attention staff members gave to patients was so generous and lifesaving. We were all allowed to express our emotions as long as they didn't create behaviors that hurt other employees or patients. The culture was collaborative, and it felt more like we were a team working on a mission together. Most of all, this was a bunch of incredibly brilliant women who had never run a business before.

And that's where I came in. Dr. Birndorf's male partner had handled all the finances, budgets, and financial modeling. He was the one who had interfaced with most of the investors. As crippled as I felt in my personal life, it was invigorating to take over The Motherhood Center's finances and other aspects of the business. (The free therapy between meetings wasn't bad either!)

It was incredible to work with a bunch of women who did not have typical "business experience" but were using their raw intelligence and intuition to put together new systems to operate the office. In my observation, these systems worked better than what had been put in place by the male partner who left. In fact, these women improved billing practices, accounts receivable collections, and major workflow issues that helped turn the business around. Sometimes these women doubted themselves, but they were incredibly thoughtful about what they were doing and made great decisions. It wasn't the easiest year, and every business has its challenges, but today The Motherhood Center is a company with multimillions of dollars of revenue. In one year, without men, we were able to turn the business from losing money to being more than profitable.

Over the course of the year, I began to realize that I had been successful in my career because I knew how to be in a man's world, get my work done, and get it done well. But this did not mean I knew how to be myself in the business world. I was good at hiding, compromising, backtracking, reading the room, and giving people what they needed. I am not saying that I never stepped on anyone's toes, but if I did, I knew how to smooth things over in order to push forward. What had seemed like a successful formula was really an approach that held me back from discovering my true power as a woman in business. Instead of being a woman trying to help people succeed in a man's world, this year would show me that I could support myself and other women to find and build success on our own terms.

Nights were tough. Days were tough. Every dark place in my mind led to another crevice where I tried to hide but couldn't. I could no longer rely on my husband for emotional support, which had always been my fallback position when the going got tough at work or with our daughters. I had to thrust myself into the world on my own and figure out how to depend on just me. I felt like I was being pounded in every direction. Yet, amid all this pain, new women kept entering my life. In fact, by September, Joan Herrmann, founder of the lifestyle brand Change Your Attitude . . . Change Your Life, invited me to join her team. I became a monthly guest on her radio show, "Conversations with Joan," which airs on New York's AM970

The Answer, streams on iHeartRadio, and is posted on all major podcast platforms.

At the time, the show felt like a lifeline. Joan had gone through a difficult divorce almost a decade earlier and was a very successful businesswoman. Her love and support, along with this new opportunity, gave me hope during a very dark time that more was possible in my own life. I also became a Reiki Master. Reiki is a type of energy healing, and I spent many wonderful, supportive, and loving afternoons with a beautiful group of women led by Cathy Towle, a shaman and Reiki master, who were to become my spiritual family. These women held me when the pain was too great and allowed me to process my emotions with love and wisdom. All my friends, too, increasingly gathered around me. And my amazing daughters were pushing forward with bravery and resilience.

I had already developed some very useful tools, especially the mindset of "maybe," which carried me on some days when I felt I could not see a future without my husband. Connecting with the fact that the future was unknown gave me the possibility that maybe things would get better, maybe I could accept this new reality and still be okay, and maybe, just maybe—though I was miserable now—I would be happy again. I started to listen to episodes of my own podcast, *10 Minutes to Less Suffering*, and felt encouraged. The podcast included topics on acceptance, gratitude, and the idea that uncertainty is our best friend. As the pain of my husband leaving me sunk in, these points that I'd been making for others became yet another lifeline. It was as if in creating these podcasts I had started sending messages to my future self, messages that would help me through. I began to see every female client I ever had in a different light. Their struggles had become my own. And for this reason, with every new client that came to me, I would never work the same way again.

I have come to realize that women today, though powerful, have no clear place to put their power. We are often referred to as either too loud or too quiet, too pretty or too ugly, too meek or too aggressive, so we are always trying to fit our power into a mold we didn't create. Most often, it never quite fits. For the first time, I saw what many of us women do in society to get along, survive, take care of our children, or just be loved. We compromise and do the best we can, but it leaves most of us less than whole and falling short of our true potential. As we are continuously persuaded to be less than our true selves, a brokenness appears in how we function each day that never really leads to our freedom. Even if we are successful in certain areas of our lives, there are places we still hide because we believe that the world will judge us harshly, that we will never be accepted for who we are, and most of all that we will never be treated as true equals at home or in the workplace.

I hesitate to share statistics about women's current status in the business world because so many of the day-to-day experiences that cause women to hide parts of themselves or that make women feel compromised, dismissed, or excluded from success cannot always be measured. But the numbers do tell an essential part of the story. As I write this book, men and women enter the workforce in equal numbers,[1] but men outnumber women nearly two to one when they reach a management position.[2] That translates to more than one million women in corporate America left behind in entry-level jobs over a five-year period.[3] Although one-third of women eventually become managers, they are often limited to mid-level positions.[4] If you look even further down the line, statistics show that only 5 percent of chief executive officers at S&P 500 companies are women.[5] Only 11 percent of the top earners at these companies are women, and only

---

1 LeanIn.Org & McKinsey, (2018). *Women in the Workplace, McKinsey & Company*, 6.

2 LeanIn.Org & McKinsey, (2018). *Women in the Workplace, McKinsey & Company*, 8.

3 Fuhrmans, V. (15 Oct 2019). Where Women Fall Behind at Work, *The Wall Street Journal*, https://www.wsj.com/articles/where-women-fall-behind-at-work-the-first-step-into-management-11571112361

4 Catalyst, *"Pyramid: Women in S&P 500 Companies"* (January 15, 2020).

5 Ibid.

20 percent of their board members are women. [6] And although four out of ten businesses in the United States are started by women,[7] only a very small percentage of them have over one million dollars in revenue[8] and less than 2.2 percent of venture capital in the United States goes to companies founded solely by women.[9] In addition, companies with all-male founders receive funding after their first round of financing close to 35 percent of the time, while for women, that number is less than 2 percent.[10]

Statistics indicating that women are not experiencing equality in the workplace abound. But none of them can ever tell the entire story of what it is like to be a woman in the workplace, nor do statistics get at the story of who we become because of these experiences and who we think we need to be to succeed. Yes, some of us have stepped out of the box, but most of us have tried to be successful by changing who we are to get along in a business environment that was not made for us. Even when we do this, the majority of us still do not have the same success as men in the business world. Although my year without men has been very painful, it has also been a gift. It has enabled me to see the path forward for women in a different way. I now see a different way to be, a new possibility not only for myself but for the women I work with and for our society as a whole.

What was the difference that has made all the difference? Since there were practically no men in my life, I had no one to please and no male model to conform to. I had no one to dress for, no one to judge me, no one to blame me, no one to say I was too emotional,

---

6 Ibid.

7 American Express OPEN, (2018). *The 2018 State of Women-Owned Business Report*, 3.

8 EY Entrepreneurial Winning Women, (2019). *Force Multipliers: How three fundamental adaptations can help women entrepreneurs scale big*, 1.

9 Zayra, V. (21 Jan 2018). Female Founders Got 2% of Venture Capital Dollars in 2017, *Fortune*, https://fortune.com/2018/01/31/female-founders-venture-capital-2017/

10 Szyvhowski, E. and Stembel, C. (8 March 2019). Women-Owned Businesses Face a Lack of Funding, *MarketWatch*, https://www.marketwatch.com/story/women-owned-businesses-face-a-lack-of-funding-and-heres-how-to-change-this-2019-03-08

no one to doubt my intelligence, no man trying to hold me back to protect his own ego, and no one to hide from. I was free.

Through that freedom, this book was born. It wasn't born from just my pain but also from twenty-seven years in the business world and in a marriage, as well as nineteen years as a mother. It was born out of a lifetime of seeing myself as "less than" in a world that, despite women's strides, is still dominated by male culture and thought. Everything from corporate structures, how we raise equity, acceptable workplace behaviors, childcare in the workplace, investing money, who predominantly raises children, and even how we conduct government affairs are mostly dominated by a male-oriented business culture. We are pushed to conform rather than bring our own greatness forward. How would we even know if the many characteristics that women generally possess and the jobs we tend to choose are really *our choices* as opposed to the effects of living in a male-dominated world? Many of us have become who we needed to be to get along in this world, which creates a tremendous amount of stress and prevents us from fostering our most innovative, creative, and prosperous selves. During my year without men, new information just poured in about how to empower myself, my daughters, and all the women I worked with so we may realize our full potential and discover our life's path. When we are free of constraints and can be our true selves, we can see our way forward to create our best lives.

To be clear, this is not a book set against men. It is a book about women developing without men, sometimes despite men, and sometimes beyond men. It is about finding those places within ourselves that we shut down because we don't feel loved or accepted, or we think we aren't smart enough or strong enough, or we don't have the same opportunities that men or even other women have had. It is about moving away from how other people should understand us and moving toward understanding ourselves. It is about redefining what beauty is, playing by our own rules, and finding a way to support ourselves spiritually, emotionally, physically, and financially in any circumstance. It is about healing, and about finding a way to become our authentic selves even when we work with men every day or in male-dominated fields. It is about embracing our true value and loving and being kind to the people we are.

We can honor our vision of how the world should be and act upon that even if that means leaving corporate America, starting our own business, going back to school, taking classes if we are home taking care of our children, and taking care of our bodies and holding space for the unique way we want to live our lives.

Over this past year, it has become abundantly clear to me that women are brilliant businesspeople and emotional warriors, but we often lose our way because of beliefs that we hold about ourselves. So, yes, there are glass ceilings and elements of the patriarchy that hold women back in today's world, but a fully empowered woman stops trying to fit into a world that is not aligned with her true nature. Some women do well in corporate America, and some women do better outside it, working for themselves. Either way, none of us can be truly successful in all areas of our lives unless we deal with our stresses, anxieties, and insecurities. We need to build our self-worth and learn to trust ourselves. We need to be totally comfortable in any room we are in, and we need to be responsible for ourselves. We cannot hide behind a man or anyone else. We need always to be able to make a living even if we choose to stay home to raise our children or for any other reason.

In the pages that follow are all the things I have discovered this year that hold women back, all the things I discovered that held me back, and all the ways I found to break free. My message is simple. Don't be afraid if you don't fit into a man's world. Don't be afraid if you see things differently. You are not crazy. You are just seeing a new world that is being born, a world where the workplace, whether you are on your own or in an office, is full of more compassion, more empathy, a greater range of emotions, free thinking, support, and creativity. A world where gender doesn't matter. But before we get there, we must believe *we* matter first.

The journey is not easy. To live a fully realized life and find our true path in a culture made for men, we have to ask hard questions. Is a forty-hour workweek the best for creating great abundance and balanced family lives? Do we need to secure clients with golf outings and fancy dinners, or is there a more creative way to reach clientele? Are there different ways to raise equity, so we don't need to be at the mercy of the lack of capital available to women? Would there be more female CEOs or more women who own multimillion-dollar businesses if we were better able to be our authentic selves in the business world? The list goes on and on. In the face of a system that doesn't work for so many of us, men and women alike, we have no choice but to pave our own way, make our own rules, love ourselves, and allow our own ideas to thrive.

My year without men gave me a whole new paradigm from which to operate. I am not saying I never spoke to any men for a year. I did have a few male friends and a wonderful father and brother and brother-in-law. Yet, for the first time in my career, I had no male clients, and for the first time in twenty-nine years, my husband was not in my life. My work life and home life were mostly supported by women, including my two beautiful daughters, my mother, sister, best friend from childhood, cousins, incredible professional mentors and guides, the women in my workplaces, and some wonderful friends and healers. Women helped me through the pain of my breakup and a serious health scare. Women were everywhere I turned, and in their presence, I felt nourished and healed.

I went from being a puddle on my kitchen floor, thinking the best I could do was make it to the wall to bang my head against it, to finding a whole new way to be in the world. I faced personal and professional upheaval and learned to rely on myself to see me through it all. If I can live a year without men, so can everyone else. I hope the lessons I learned can inspire other women to open new businesses, find new jobs, thrive economically, create new cures for diseases, go back to school, or start a side business while they are home taking care of their children. This is not about whether or not you are involved with men. Instead, it is about divesting yourself from other people's ideas of who you need to be or how you need to operate, and it can be an entirely internal process. It's about becoming fully realized, so every choice we make is not from fear but from strength. We can create our own institutions from within, and they will be reflected on the outside. When our own voices matter to us, we can succeed as parents, entrepreneurs, industry leaders, and innovators.

It is doable. I have done it. I have spent an entire year holding myself up, holding other women up, and being held by a bunch of incredible women. We are all so wise when we let ourselves be who we truly are, and trust our thoughts, and trust our dreams. This book is based on my beliefs and ideas that have grown out of my own personal experiences. I realize that women from different communities, both here and around the world, have different experiences and encounter different roadblocks based on their race, ethnicity, socio-economic background, sexuality, and other factors. My hope for this book is that no matter who you are, where you come from, or what you have faced in your life, some of my ideas and beliefs will inspire you to embrace your best creative, authentic, and abundant life.

Chapter 1: July
Make Friends with Uncertainty

"Uncertainty is the refuge of hope."

—Henri Frederic Amiel

***

WHEN I think back to the beginning of my separation from my husband, I can't decide which was harder: his actually leaving me or being in counseling together for seven weeks. Sitting in counseling with someone whom I'd had to beg to stay was overwhelmingly painful. There was something so awful about someone who had been my best friend the month before who was now so cold and distant, who was only sitting through therapy, it seemed, as a concession to me.

In therapy, we "explored" why he wanted to leave. But the reason was simple. He wanted to date other people. I watched him struggle to come up with a better explanation, but this, in the end, was what it came down to. What were the chances counseling could shift that? In counseling, one of the hardest parts was living with the uncertainty of whether the marriage could be saved.

One night, as I lay in bed crying while my husband slept next to me, I noticed my book *The Gift of Maybe* on my nightstand. I picked it up and went into the bathroom, where I sat with my legs out in front of me on the cold tile floor. I opened up the book and started to read. I had begun writing the book in 2011, and it was now seven years later. As I read through the first chapter, which explored the kinds of fears I'd been living with for years, to my surprise, I found that I had listed "Would my husband always love me?" as one of my fears. The words hit me hard. It was as if I had been writing to my future self, reminding her to embrace this mindset of maybe when the time came, and I'd really need it.

The premise of *The Gift of Maybe* is that being addicted to certainty creates fear and limits what is possible in our lives. It was born from my experience that if I didn't know what would happen next in my life, I projected things would be bad and not work out. I was unable to sit in the uncertainty of life and be open to all the possible outcomes, especially the good ones.

As I held the published book in my hands now, I remembered when I was writing it that I came across a quote by the great philosopher Jiddhu Krishnamurti who, when sharing his secret to happiness, said, "Do you want to know what my secret is? I don't mind what happens." It is simple to understand why this state of mind leads to freedom and happiness: if we don't mind what happens next in our lives, we have no reason to be stressed and worried today. Although not minding is a ticket to emotional freedom, most of us cannot help but care about what will happen next in our lives. We care about keeping our jobs, having enough money, our children being healthy, being in good relationships, our spouse or boyfriend or girlfriend not breaking up with us, and a slew of other crucial outcomes. We want to make sure that the things we want to happen actually do happen—and that is precisely where our need for certainty begins. Yet we can't control everything, and life is filled with twists and turns; sometimes our efforts to secure certainty leave us far from the life that we desire. Do we mind? Absolutely.

I was addicted to certainty for most of my adult life until one day, I heard this story about a farmer and his horse. The story goes like this. One day, a farmer's horse ran away. His neighbor came by and said, "You have the worst luck."

The farmer replied to the neighbor, "Maybe."

The next day, the horse returned with five mares, and his neighbor came by and said, "You have the best luck."

The farmer replied, "Maybe."

The day after that, the farmer's son was riding the horse and fell off and broke his leg, and the neighbor came by and said to the farmer, "You have the worst luck."

The farmer replied, "Maybe." The next day, the army came looking to draft the boy for combat, but he could not go because his leg was broken.

The neighbor came by and said, "You have the best luck."

Again, the farmer said, "Maybe."

Even in the midst of the most painful moment of my life, this story again provided an opening. This time, it didn't alleviate the pain immediately as it had the first time I encountered it. The pain in my heart was just too deep right now. But the story did give me a glimmer of hope.

As I read my book, I came upon the exercise in the first chapter. I got a pen from my bedroom and returned to the bathroom floor. Hunched over, on a blank page in my book, I wrote the question down that I had asked so many of my clients before, "What is your biggest fear?" I was quite certain of my answer. I was afraid my husband was really leaving me, not just saying he wanted to, and that the pain would kill me. I was afraid that I would never survive and never have a joyful life again. I was afraid for my daughters. I was afraid that they would crumble and become weak, insecure women. I feared that they would never be happy again. And then I asked myself, "Am I absolutely sure these fears are true?" This was a question I had answered so many times before, but here I was afraid to say what came next. Still, I knew in my soul what the answer was: I didn't know that my fears about the future were true. My life had maybe.

I curled into a fetal position and kept writing. As I lay on the bathroom floor, I couldn't even lift my head to watch the pen in my hand writing on the page. I just wrote maybe statement after maybe statement. I could barely catch my breath. The statements were illegible, each written over the next. I cried and screamed as I wrote them. My husband never came to knock on the door.

I wrote for thirty minutes. Maybe my husband and I would work it out. Maybe we would have a happy marriage. Maybe we would heal the wounds this had caused. I also recognized that maybe I could accept whatever was going to happen and still be okay. Maybe there would be a life for me beyond all of this, even though I could not think of one. Then, I kept writing again and again: Maybe everything is okay; Maybe everything is okay; Maybe everything is okay. My mind recognized that there was maybe. But I felt no light in my heart that night. I did fall asleep for a few hours on the bathroom floor. It was the first time I had slept in days.

I continued this ritual every night. We were in counseling, so I thought we were trying to save our marriage. I leaned toward maybe scenarios that had us staying together, but I also spent as much time on maybe statements that did not include us being together. All day long, I repeated to myself in my head: *Maybe everything will be okay.*

During this time while I wasn't sleeping and everything was up and down, Dr. Catherine Birndorf asked me to join The Motherhood Center. In deciding to split with her business partner, who was a male, she asked me to give the company more time. I was in pretty bad shape, but I had done so many maybe statements every night that these words fell out of my mouth in response to her invitation: "Maybe I can give you more time"; "Maybe this would be good for me"; "Maybe it's a good idea I earn more money right now, especially since my biggest client for the past twenty-five years is in the process of selling his business and my marriage is headed I don't know where." The truth was, I didn't have a real interest in working at the Center, but my maybe work made The Motherhood Center seem like a place of possibility. Could life be pulling me forward, despite my desire to hang on to how things had always been?

I performed my work well but, as I mentioned in the introduction, I was crying to Dr. Birndorf in between the meetings. At one point, she took *The Gift of Maybe* from her shelf and started to use it as her mouse pad. From then on, I couldn't sit in the room without seeing my book. One day she and I were talking in between meetings. She was at her computer. My eyes fell on the book, and she followed my gaze. "Let me ask you something, Allison," she said. "Do you think everyone has *maybe*?"

Without hesitation, I responded, "I know they do."

"Then so do you," she said to me with a smile and in a tone of expertise and authority.

There was something about that moment. It was as if my maybe prayers had been reflected back at me. Yes, if every client of mine and everyone who read my book and beyond had maybe, then so did I. The thought didn't move my pain, but when I heard it from this strong, capable woman, finally the light of hope entered my heart. It was slight but palpable. I had one of the lead psychiatrists in the world reflecting maybe back to me. Not so bad!

When Dr. Birndorf was treating a patient that day, I found an empty office, and I closed my eyes for a few minutes. I was immediately reminded of a friend from years ago. I had given him my book to read a few weeks after his wife died, and he came up to me a few weeks after that and told me he hated it. He said his wife had died and that his life had no maybe. I was so upset. I thought I had crossed the boundaries of maybe and, most of all, our friendship. It bothered me for a long time. But after some time had passed, this friend approached me again. "I have to say, I loved your book," he told me. "Six months after my wife died, I said to myself, 'Maybe there is still something left for me to experience in this lifetime.' Now, I have a girlfriend. It doesn't mean I am happier, or I love her more than I did my wife, but I am making the most of every day and seeing where maybe takes me." Like my friend, in that moment at The Motherhood Center at the end of July 2018, eyes closed and still reeling from pain, I thought to myself, *Maybe there is something left for me to experience in this lifetime.*

I finally felt some hope that maybe everything would be okay no matter what happened. I was weak and heartbroken, but I knew that uncertainty was my best friend. I stayed close to

my breath so that I could stay grounded in each moment and muttered "maybe" each and every day.

* * *

It might seem like a leap from my personal story of loss to a discussion of women in the business world, but bear with me. I have been in the business world for the last twenty-seven years in New York City. There aren't many women I know of in this city who, like me, were attorneys at a large law firm, then had their own law firm, and then transitioned to business coach/consultant and life strategist. I've had many different male and female clients in different industries. I've helped people grow their businesses, and as time went on also focused on my clients' emotional and spiritual growth. I've also helped women through divorce, ironically, and coached parents and anyone who needed my help. Over the past twenty-seven years, for the people I've worked with, hands down the biggest source of stress and worry or lack of success was exactly what was plaguing me during the month of July when my marriage teetered in the balance—a deep fear of the unknown.

Do women fear uncertainty more than men? No. This fear of uncertainty—hurray for equality!—is shared equally by men and women. But because men still have more of an advantage in the business world and society in general, women's fear of the unknown creates more roadblocks and chaos in our lives when we let this fear derail us.

I know things have gotten better for women over the years, but we are far from being on equal footing with men. Yes, women earn more than they ever have in the past. We start more businesses and hold more management positions. But we are a long way from having equivalent opportunities and advantages to men in the business world. Women still need to work harder in the corporate world to succeed. We have to be more creative to balance our lives with children and family. Less is handed to us on a silver platter. On top of it all, if we fear the unknown, we severely limit what is possible for us in the world of business and beyond.

When I was an attorney working at a large law firm many years ago, men were more likely to inherit clients from a male partner, better able to bond over sports, dating, and trips to the bar, and didn't often leave the workplace for a few years to raise kids and ask for part-time work. To deal with these inequities, every woman I have met along the way had to be smarter, more efficient, and more controlled with their emotions than most men I have met. And the same is true for the female clients I know who navigate the work world today. This is where the fear of the unknown comes into play.

Life seems so much more uncertain with no clear road to success when you struggle to have your voice heard. Yet if we fear the unknown, we often stay with what we think is safe and secure, hewing to a narrow path toward what we believe is best for our future. If we are in a male-dominated industry, those safer opportunities are limited and might not lead to the full career path we had in mind when we started our journey. For me, even my choice to become a tax attorney was rooted in my need for certainty and to feel valued by others. I felt safe with numbers because numbers don't lie—unless someone embezzles from a company and alters the financial records. My father told me I would make a good living because people would always need me. I believed that becoming a tax attorney was securing my future, even if that choice had nothing to do with my passions or true goals for my life.

Yet, there was actually no safety in becoming a tax attorney. This I learned on my second day of work. I was told the firm where I was working would be firing half of the first years at the law firm. I was a first year. By the end of the year, they didn't fire me, but they did fire my friend who had graduated law school with me. My illusion of safety in any particular job would never return. I was at a job I didn't like, and I didn't even have the security that I had yearned for my entire life. So, even if we choose a path that seems "safer," many of us find out at some point that nothing is a sure thing, that all the sacrifices we made might not have left us very secure at all.

This is quite a conundrum for women. We look for places to feel safe because we don't always feel life is fair or that we have the same opportunities as men, but choices made out of our need for safety can eventually leave us short of achieving our goals, living our authentic lives, and truly expressing who we are.

For me, corporate America was stifling. And when I meet women who stayed in corporate America or who are in their twenties and thirties, their stories don't seem that different from mine. There are more women in the workplace, but many of the behaviors that target, disadvantage, and harm women continue. No one can pretend that sexual harassment or exploitation is a thing of the past. And other bad behaviors on the part of men—from passing women up for promotions and not listening to women in meetings to denying women-led businesses access to funding—may be more subtle and more lawful, but they are rampant, nonetheless.

I spoke with a friend the other day who stayed on the partnership track of a law firm since she and I left law school to take our first jobs. Now a partner, she told me that everything is okay because she sticks close to other women at her firm. Although I appreciate her success, why should we be in an office environment where we need to "stick" to anyone in order to flourish or even just to survive? Why do we need to be protected by other women when our skills are just as good as those of the men doing the same jobs?

We all know the answer. The system is still made for men. Women are trying to fit into a system that was not made for them. The contrast is stark when women create their own systems. At The Motherhood Center, the rules of the business were built for the women who work there. For example, years ago, I consulted for a male client with a large company. When one of his female employees got pregnant, he told me there was a sense that this employee wouldn't be committed to the business in the same way. No one at the company ever bothered to figure out how this woman could have more work-life balance that still left her in a leadership position. Only one level of commitment was tolerated, and that came with no room for any other priority. At The Motherhood Center, by contrast, it was simply understood that women have children. We expect that some people who work at the Center will work only three or four days a week or, if they work five days, they might leave at three o'clock to pick their child up at school. Yes, some people work full days, but the Center considers the quality of life and quality of work, and not just hours punched on a time clock. (And, yes, we are currently profitable!)

It is unrealistic for businesses to continue operating within the confines of the existing workweek with so many women in the workplace, especially given how expensive and inaccessible childcare can be. How can we expect our society to be a place of equality, for children to be cared for, and for families to flourish when we don't allow for change? There is a continued bias against men being the primary caregivers, and single women face sizable stigma of their own. Now, don't get me wrong, there are many women who are able to work full-time and care for a family and do it beautifully. And single women, with or without children, can also succeed in corporate America. I am just saying that instead of a few women succeeding by conforming to the perceived needs of corporate America's male-dominated executives, the system as a whole should shift to recognize the needs of women and allow us all to approach work with more flexibility. A better focus for companies would be on a balanced lifestyle for all employees, which I would argue makes for better communities, innovation, and business profitability.

This is not a tangent from the discussion of uncertainty. If we fear the unknown, it is hard to leave behind what we know. It is hard for a company to create a corporate culture that values employees' family time equally to their work time. It is hard on an individual level for a woman to leave a corporate job that pays well even though it does not align with her true self or her desire for work-life balance. It is hard for women to raise capital and for investors to see women-owned businesses as just as capable of generating profit as male-owned businesses. It is hard for women to leave the workplace to raise their children and return at competitive salaries without the same opportunities that their male counterparts have. And the list goes on.

In order to change the system, our fear of the unknown must be cast aside and we must envision a life that works for us and believe in its possibilities. In order to seize our full equality, we must be willing *not* to know. We must be willing to take risks that will lead us to new possibilities that work for our lives. Our relationship with the unknown is the key to shifting to a more equitable society with equal pay and opportunities and economic growth for women.

It might seem too simple that a little word like maybe is going to change the world. How is it possible that *maybe* can reduce your stress and worry, help you find the resilience to pursue your goals, go back to school, or even start a business? How is it possible that it will make you stronger in your personal relationships and ensure that you don't settle for safety but instead look for greatness? How is it possible that *maybe* can alter the landscape of the workplace?

The mindset of maybe reminds you that you are never stuck, that everything you don't know is not your enemy, and instead, uncertainty is your best friend because that is where your life will change. Maybe is a tool for growth, resilience, and strength for every woman to look outside everything that she has ever been told and find her own way.

Maybe reminds us that the past has no bearing on what is possible if we stay open, work hard, and recognize that no matter what happens, life has maybe. Businesses can be challenging, relationships present obstacles, and twists and turns lead us astray each day. But maybe reminds us that maybe whatever we are experiencing is good, maybe it can get better, and maybe we can accept what we are experiencing and still be okay. Maybe there is something new coming our way, maybe the answers will come. And the list goes on and on. In truth, until our last breath, we have maybe. There is no reason to give up when Maybe is by your side.

If we can find the courage to face the unknown, we can "not mind" our futures, or at least mind them a bit less. We can examine new ideas, go to places we never expected to go, or develop a relationship with someone different from us. We can boldly raise capital for businesses, go back to school, speak up when we are the only woman in the room, and not fall apart when the men we love leave us.

Our paths as women seem less certain than those laid out for men, especially if we choose to have children and work, but we must remember that nobody has certainty. Instead, all we have is possibility. And even though this moment, whatever it is, might seem to offer a man greater possibility, we often forget that we are looking at this moment with the eyes of the past, with the eyes of everything that has been taught to us, of what we cannot have and what will limit us.

It is time for women to recognize that many of us are still supporting a system created long ago even though it doesn't work for us. Many people call it the patriarchy, a social system in which men hold the power and all others are largely denied access to. If we fear the unknown, it is impossible to break out of the patriarchy and shift the balance of power to achieve more equality. It is tough to break out of a mold when there is no clear road ahead. But everything we want as women—whether it is to become CEO of a big company, start our own business, save the environment, create a more peaceful world, make a good living, or stay at home and take care of our kids—cannot be achieved if we believe in any source of security outside of ourselves. If we look for certainty in the world around us, we will live in fear; we will never seize the life that we want for ourselves, our children, and our world.

Uncertainty is our best friend. We sometimes fear change, but if we recognize that all change contains maybe, we can bring a more hopeful perspective into our future. The truth is plain and clear:

if you want your life to change, it has to happen in the unknown future. So, equality for all women—and with it equal opportunities, better access to health care, greater political involvement, and more economic stability, among many other things—must happen in the unknown. And maybe, just maybe, it is possible. It is certainly not possible if we continue to think nothing will change.

Every time we quit our jobs in corporate America to start a business, we have maybe by our side. Every time we get married and have kids, we have maybe by our side. Every time we keep our skills current and start a side business when our children are small, we are embracing maybe. Every time we go back to school, launch a second career, or even go through a divorce or a second marriage, all of that has maybe in it. In reality, maybe is the hope within the unknown.

I recently watched Melinda Gates on a Super Soul Sunday episode with Oprah. Ms. Gates told Oprah that in the work she does for the Gates foundation abroad, she often has to deal with men in developing nations. In these places, men usually have the power to decide what happens for women in their countries. The example she used was about helping women access contraceptives and how men often stand in the way of this. Many of us in developed countries see ourselves as liberated. We don't have to go through our husbands or fathers for permission to access contraception, for example. But the patriarchy still controls how we see ourselves, how we beat ourselves up psychologically, how limited we feel, and how corporate rules are made by men.

Many of us don't speak up about how we are treated, dismissed, looked over, and not valued. We don't speak about how we are overworked and stressed and have no work-life balance for ourselves and our families because we fear retribution or losing our jobs or rocking the boat of our relationships. But in truth, we fear uncertainty. We see leaving the mainstream or speaking up against what's not working as a risk. We are unable to accept that the unknown future could offer us other opportunities that are most authentic to who we are. We fail to see the maybe. The patriarchy encourages a worldview that is very matter of fact. If you can't see it, it doesn't exist, we are told. But this fallacy is man's creation. It is time that women embrace the idea of maybe. We need to stop thinking about how the world is and, as Gandhi said, "Be the change you want to see in the world."

This is about creating new corporate structures, new types of businesses, new family dynamics, and new ways to take care of each other. The only way to begin this journey is not to fear the unknown, not to fear the new approaches that women come to bear when they have a voice. Some of us still hide behind men for a security that is false. Those of us who have been left see this falsehood clear as day. Our safety does not lie in a man or in our shared bank accounts but instead in our authentic self and in finding our voice and path. I have seen women start incredible businesses and stand up for themselves in different companies, creating new paradigms. But if we fear uncertainty, we will always reach for the world that we have been sold as unchangeable when it is not. This world tells us how we have to look, what we have to do, how we must act, and how we can be taken care of, and this is a false reality. The world we are in is one that desperately needs women to start taking care of things.

Uncertainty is every woman's ticket to freedom, but we must realize that all we don't know will reveal itself over time. We need to create a society where women can work and have a balanced family life and not a society that *tolerates* women having babies and working. As I previously mentioned, I can't tell you how many times over the years I've heard the male head of a company make a crack about a woman employee's productivity when she has a baby or how many times I have watched a woman eventually get fired or demoted because she had a child. Watching the news, women in sports commercials, or *The View*, you can believe that we are making strides. We are. But as we progress further, we will be limited if we are addicted to certainty or can't manage the risk of not knowing.

For me, in the month of July, with my marriage and the life I had built hanging by a thread, one word was saving me. As it had for years, one word helped me continue to grow my business, do a podcast, go on the radio, cultivate corporate clients, work with anyone who came my way, and become CFO of The Motherhood Center, a position that I have never held before. That word was and is still *maybe*. Maybe reminds me that I don't need to know all the answers. Instead, I need to quiet my fear and understand myself and my path, embracing the many possibilities in my unknown future.

Try This Exercise: Maybe Everything Is Okay

Here is the exercise I did that alleviated so much of my emotional suffering. First, spend a few minutes thinking about a current situation that is causing you stress and worry. Write down a statement about how you feel about it. Now ask yourself, are your worries and stressful thoughts absolute? Can you know for certain how things will turn out for your job, marriage, business, or any other situation that is creating stress or worry in your life? If you are not certain, try to acknowledge that other possibilities may exist. Next, challenge your statement with the idea of maybe. Write down the following: Maybe my beliefs about my situation are not true; Maybe what is happening is good; Maybe what is happening can get better; Maybe I can find a way to accept whatever I am experiencing and find a way to make the best of it; Maybe there is something left to experience in this moment; Maybe, in time, I will know what to do next; Maybe everything is okay.

You can put these statements in your own words or just use the ones that feel right. You can also create maybe statements regarding specific action steps that you might consider taking regarding your issue. How does your situation look against the idea of maybe? Do you feel more hopeful? Do you see that the situation can work out differently than you feared it would?

Write these statements of yours a few times each day and review them often. If you can, add more maybe statements that challenge your stress and worry about the current situation. Keep your attention on these maybe statements over the next few days and see what happens to your stress and worry. As you start to feel a shift, add the following as you finish reciting your maybe statements: "I am available and willing to see the situation differently." Each situation you face and each new venture has many possible outcomes. Some of them might be different and, indeed, even better than you imagined.

Chapter 2: August
Accept That You Can't Stop the Rain

"For after all, the best thing one can do when it is raining,
is to let it rain."

—Henry Wadsworth Longfellow

* * *

As we sat in marriage counseling, I felt everything slipping away. My husband's complaints were expanding. He was bringing up things from so long ago that I couldn't remember them, much less explain my side of them. Didn't he see the woman sitting next to him now? He brought up things like: "Well, we went to her parents' house every weekend when we first got married." This, from over twenty-seven years ago! Or "I stayed in the city to go to graduate school to be with her when I didn't want to." That, over twenty-nine years ago! It began to dawn on me that he had already made his decision and was looking for justification to support his intention of leaving his family to have sex with other women.

I remember our last marriage counseling session so vividly. I had a pit in my stomach, and I stopped at Starbucks near the therapist's office. I called my best friend Robin, as I had before every session. She picked up, as she always does.

I have to take a minute to thank this beautiful woman. If you have a best friend like Robin, you know what it means. I am blessed to have her in my life. She has been my best friend through thick and thin. We met when we were five years old at summer camp and bonded over orange popsicles and kickball games. Little did we know that we were embarking on a lifetime friendship supporting each other through joy and heartbreak. When you have a friend that stands by you, this friendship is like a magic cord when you lose your way.

"I think he's going to end therapy today," I told Robin. We have been friends for such a long time that although she was still in shock about what was happening to my marriage, she knew that when I have a pit in my stomach (we all have intuitive ways that our bodies react), real trouble was brewing. But the truth was, you didn't have to be a psychic to see the writing on the wall. Over the weekend, while we were picking out costumes for my friend's Australian-themed birthday party in a few weeks, my husband turned to me and said, "You know, this might not work out." He became panicked that our older daughter would leave for college before we might be able to tell her that we were separating. I realize now that he was never planning on going to this party with me, but in that moment, all I could think about was that he had promised to stay in therapy for at least three months—we were only halfway through.

I will spare you the brutal details, but it felt like I was trying to stop a giant wave coming right at me. Sure enough, as we sat in therapy later that day, he announced that he wanted to separate. The therapist tried to slow it down. She told us that we had more between us than most people who come into her office; maybe we should let the week go by and reconsider it next week. She indicated that there was a lot at stake, so we should be thoughtful about this. But my husband was clear in that he wanted to dissolve the marriage. The session ended abruptly.

We walked the three miles home in blistering heat. Along the way, I pleaded with him to save our marriage. But he was already talking about how to tell the kids and how we would manage the money. He also told me I would be fine tomorrow because I had all my friends and family. He said I should have replaced the bedspread in our bedroom over two years ago—it really upset him. His eyes were glazed over, and there was an incoherence to everything he was saying in such an important and dramatic moment in both of our lives, but he was clear about one thing: our marriage was over.

I had entered a state of shock and couldn't believe my ears. What had happened? What life did he know other than his life with his family? What had I missed? This ending was a maybe that I knew had been possible, but in my heart of hearts had not thought probable. As we walked, my head started to swirl. This actually felt like the end of my life. It was only the thought *Maybe everything will be okay* that got me home.

Without a doubt, the only thing worse than my husband leaving me was telling our two daughters. Like me and every single person in my life other than my husband, the girls had no idea that this was coming. My husband went to bed early with a cold, and I was up late with the girls. We were talking about this and that, but I could barely breathe. My older daughter was pressuring me about weekend plans because she wanted to see her boyfriend, but I knew that we wouldn't make it to the weekend as a family still intact. Right then, I blurted out, "Dad and I are separating. He is no longer happy in the marriage."

Both of our girls froze. I watched their innocence break in front of me. It was as if I were watching their dreams crushed under rubble as the idea and feeling of unconditional love and family ceased to feed their sense of safety in the world.

I immediately ran to wake up my husband so he could speak to them, too, but chaos had erupted. He had wanted us to follow his own plan to tell the children in a way that suited him and his departure. He wanted friendship, family vacations, and family holidays.

But he wanted something he could not have. He wanted the three of us to accept his decision and understand, but he was destroying the most important thing in all of our lives: our precious family that the girls and I treasured. I did my best that night. I've thought a lot about it, but I honestly don't think I could have sat through a planned discussion with the children. The shock and chaos were too much for me to hold. I actually think I would have said some awful things had I been present listening to him tell the girls his reasons for leaving. For me, this was best. I think for the children, this was best. I said very little at the time, and he had an opportunity to speak to them on his own. For some reason, he decided to share with my older daughter many of the details of why he wanted to leave that next day. He told her things he never even told me.

In the months to follow, he blamed me often for the way we had told them and how it all would have been different if we had followed his plan. It was as if my husband thought he could control where all the pieces of a bomb explosion would land. I went to therapy for six months and brought this issue up often. Had I been wrong to blurt out the news? My therapist would always look at me and say, "That is the least important thing about what happened at the end of your marriage."

A year later, I would ask my older daughter about that night. She laughed at me, and said, "Mom, do you really think, whether you told us, or you and dad told us together, it would have changed how we felt about the fact that he was leaving? Oh, please!" Once my children knew, there was no going back. Everything happened quickly. By my twenty-seventh wedding anniversary on August 24, my children and I left the city, and my husband moved out.

As I've described, the night of my anniversary, I took off my ring and felt my whole world crumble around me. But something happened the next day that I will also never forget. I remember waking up, turning to my right, and seeing that my husband was not there next to me. He hadn't gone to work out or ride his bike. He would never again be at my side when I woke up. I don't know if I was trying to punish myself or was just in shock, but I kept turning my head again to the right, then closing my eyes and opening them. I kept acknowledging that he was not there. I did it again and again. There was something about the repetition as if I were trying to accept it, but I couldn't.

In an attempt to stop this obsessive loop, I went to take a shower. I turned on the water and waited for the temperature to adjust while it ran. The shower was in a bathtub, so as I prepared to step in, I moved slowly. Right before stepping under the stream of water, I noticed that the shower sounded like rain. This immediately reminded me of the Henry Longfellow quote, "For after all, the best thing one can do when it is raining, is to let it rain."

Let it rain. At that moment, I felt a definite release. It wasn't that I thought to myself, *Oh, I got this. I accept this.* It was more that the swirl inside me, the part that had been trying to get back where I was before the end of June, just dissipated. It was done. It was raining, and I couldn't control the rain.

As I learned in the months to come, it would be much easier to accept what I did that day—that my husband was not physically present in my life anymore—than to accept that my marriage, the emotions, and the bond we had shared were gone, too, and that nothing would ever be the same. But it was a start.

There is something about *not* accepting a situation that creates a free fall. There is no bottom to our pain because we keep arguing about what is happening, which brings us deeper and deeper into chaos. In the shower, I just kept thinking, *I can't control the rain.* The situation was still unbearable, but at that moment, I stopped trying to go back in time to erase what had happened. As I got out of the shower and started to dry off, another quote came to me, and I actually said it out loud. I knew the words well because both my daughters had each played Lady Macbeth in their respective fourth grade productions. At the time, I thought they were a bit young for such mature productions, but they had both made compelling Lady Macbeths in their American Girl Roman satin dresses.

As I stood there on the shower mat toweling off, I started to say over and over again, as Lady Macbeth had while sleepwalking, "What's done cannot be undone." I knew there was no turning back. I would go insane if over time I didn't at least accept the fact that my husband had left, and my marriage was over.

***

Why is acceptance so important for women in business, in relationships, and in every other aspect of our lives? Because other than uncertainty, a lack of acceptance is what causes the most amount of pain in our lives and wastes most of our time. Time is a resource that no one in business, least of all women, can afford to waste.

I do not approach the topic of acceptance lightly. Even though I gained some type of acceptance about my marriage that day, there were many more levels of acceptance that I needed to achieve afterward. Still, all of it started with the acceptance of the fact that he had left, and he wasn't coming back.

It's completely understandable why acceptance can be a difficult concept for some people because it is about tolerating or making peace with something that we don't like or which causes us pain both physically and emotionally. Also, the world around us is often telling us to focus on overcoming our problems and persevering at all costs until we achieve our goals. Many of us believe this means that we should not accept things in our lives that we don't like, but this is the biggest misconception about the idea of acceptance. When you accept something, it does not mean that you will stop trying to make your life better or give up on achieving your goals. It doesn't mean that you will necessarily stop having emotions about the situation. Instead, acceptance is about not arguing with reality. It's about letting go of the pain that we experience when we resist what is happening.

In my experience, both men and women have equal trouble accepting things, especially in business. Whether it's a job loss, a financial loss when the markets take a downturn, other unsuccessful investments, or—the most difficult—a failed business, none of us want to accept defeat. However, just as the fear of the unknown can disproportionately affect women because we have more difficulty achieving complete equality in the workplace, not accepting things quickly can also become a significant liability for women. Lack of acceptance also adds a tremendous amount of stress to women's already overscheduled, highly competitive work lives, tipping the work-life balance.

There are different types of acceptance that we can learn to implement in our lives. The two that I deal with the most are what I call "out-of-control acceptance" and "problem acceptance." I will not focus here on accepting things like a life-threatening illness or the loss of a loved one because this book focuses more on relationships, business issues, and day-to-day stress. That said, while more care is needed when a situation is acute and life threatening, these concepts can be applied to any situation. For now, I want to focus on the resistance we have to common issues in our personal and business lives and how we can use acceptance techniques to reduce our suffering and find more peace, joy, and success.

First, let's home in on what I call out-of-control acceptance. It might seem difficult based on the name, but this is the easiest form of acceptance. Most of us don't realize that all day long we are arguing with so many little things that we have no control over. We let these little things get us stressed, or we allow them to change our mood, which can carry over to the rest of our day without even realizing it. We could be sitting in traffic, and we might get angry that we'll be late for an important meeting. Or we could be forced to wait for someone else who is late. The Internet could be slow at a café, we might be in a long line at a store, or on hold for a long time with a customer service representative. Our child's room could be messy again, or there might be crumbs all over the kitchen floor. We start getting upset because things are not what we thought they would or should be. Whether we don't like waiting, we are late, or we feel we are wasting our time, whatever it is, things are not going as planned.

But being upset is just resisting what is happening whether you like it or not. This is why we need out-of-control acceptance. You can still feel angry or frustrated, but the realization that you cannot change the situation helps you get to the conclusion quickly that if you cannot control the situation, no matter how you try, you can choose a different response. The minute you choose acceptance, you are choosing a more thoughtful, productive, and peaceful approach in the face of any challenge.

For after all, the best thing one can do when it is raining, is to let it rain. It makes perfect sense. We don't think we can control the rain, but for some reason we get upset about things like traffic—as if that were ever in our control! And believe me, I live in New York City, so I have been late for more than a few meetings because I am sitting in traffic or delayed on the subway. Whether I'm upset or uptight or annoyed does not make any difference to getting me where I need to go—it's like trying to stop the rain. I'd rather find peace and enjoy the moment as best I can. So, the minute you recognize a situation is totally out of your control, that is your signal to let go and make the best of what is happening. And this approach makes all the difference in business and our relationships. When we hold on even to little things, it affects our mood. We get short-tempered and lose focus on what is important. And everyone around us sees it. It is best to come to each moment with as little baggage as possible. This approach will leave you with a clear mind and create more room for new ideas. Acceptance of what is out of your control can also help you be more open to those around you.

The next type of acceptance I'd like to discuss is problem acceptance. Problem acceptance is tricky because when you have a problem, you might be able to do something to solve it in the near or far future. But let's not confuse arguing with the fact that a problem exists with actually solving the problem or making a change. Some of us have a tendency to go over a problem in our minds again and again like a broken record. Hundreds of people in business have told me stories of not being able to sleep because they were running a business problem over and over in their minds. Business clients would tell me stories of obsessing at night about decisions that led to lost profits, client problems, missed opportunities, and employees who were under-performing or employees that were great who left for a competitor. People have also told me stories of replaying a break-up conversation or trying to undo in their minds something they did that they regret. We all have trouble sometimes believing a situation is happening that we don't want to be true, so we keep analyzing how it happened and how it could have been different. But repeating things over and over in our minds and to our friends, coworkers, and anyone else that will listen to our problem can prevent us from moving forward. Arguing with reality just keeps you in the same pain you were in the first time you learned about the issue causing you suffering.

I know things that happen in business can be shocking some-times. We might think a job is our job and it goes to someone else. A long-standing client can go to a competitor. A great business prod-uct can fail. We cannot get financing for our dream business. Or someone we trusted at work deceives us by repeating something said in confidence or not backing us up on a business decision made together. Problem acceptance does not mean you are saying you like what is happening, that you wanted it to happen, or that you won't try to change it. Instead, problem acceptance gives you the opportu-nity to reduce your pain and to be present and open to what *is* . . . and also what can be. It feels so wonderful to let go of fighting with reality even when we don't like what is happening. We think the fight is part of the change, but the fight is part of the distraction, especially in business. We need to accept reality in order to move forward and create an environment that works for us as women.

I have seen the business world be very tough on women and how they react "emotionally" to situations. I have seen men lose their tem-pers and be rude and hold grudges and carry out vendettas, but no one usually questions men's competence, even if their behavior is reprimanded. On the other hand, I have witnessed women be judged that "they are too emotional," "they don't have what it takes," "they

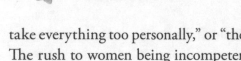

take everything too personally," or "they are impossible to work with." The rush to women being incompetent, unstable, or not qualified is unfortunate but common. Because these perceptions exist, women need to be diligent about acceptance and move toward problem-solving mode as quickly as they can. The double standard isn't fair, but quite honestly, it is a better, less painful, and more productive way to live in general when we accept things as they are.

As I discuss in a later chapter, there is nothing wrong with your feelings and emotions, and I don't take issue with feelings and emotions in the workplace if expressed in a responsive manner. You can also have emotions about a situation or a coworker and still accept the situation as a reality. I also believe that judgments about women being "too emotional" are often not even accurate and are more about sexism, misogyny, and the patriarchy than they are about women's capabilities. I have met such highly intelligent, competent, and visionary women who I believe have often been judged unfairly by their male counterparts. In fact, I find men much more emotional than women in the workplace because anger, stress responses, physical confrontations, inappropriate behavior, and screaming all stem from emotions. Of course, I have worked with some great men, and there are men in the workplace who can be more emotionally balanced than their female coworkers, but on a whole I find that women are more thoughtful, empathic, and that they lash out less than men. This is my opinion, formed from my twenty-seven years of experience in the business world, and I stand by it!

All that said, if we accept things quickly, part of our emotional reaction to a situation will be diminished, and our behaviors will reflect that. Clear minded, we will go into a productive problem-solving behavior without much delay and be sharper as we move forward with better solutions. Thus, I find that acceptance is one of the most essential qualities of an entrepreneur, businesswoman, or front-line employee at a company. Business is always about presence and creating a new future. Without acceptance, we obsess about the past without coming up with solutions. The past can create the problem and has lessons to teach us, but the business world waits for no one. We can tell stories our entire life about what has happened to us, and that very well might be true, but if we want to have real economic impact in our lives, we need to find a way to turn the problem into wisdom and move forward.

For women in the business world, acceptance doesn't mean that we are accepting less for ourselves or compromising our values or dreams for our careers or businesses or even our personal relationships. Acceptance is not about suppressing our emotions and in no way diminishes our desire for equality or our voices at a company, board room, or in our families. It is literally just acknowledging what is happening in the moment and not resisting what is right in front of us. The sooner we ask ourselves what we are going to do about what is happening, the more we will be able to compete and succeed in any room we enter. Don't get me wrong. Sometimes problem acceptance means filing a claim against a coworker with human resources at your firm, having a difficult conversation with your boss about how you believe you are being treated poorly, or even quitting your job. But often, all of that is better than repeating a story over and over in your head and not accepting that your current circumstance exists. There is a world out there waiting for you. You can push forward through your past experiences to create a path that works for you. But if you are carrying fifty pounds on your back, it will be hard to compete, create, and find your place.

As I said at the beginning of this chapter, this is not always easy. I can't even tell you how many nights I lay awake, trying to undo what had been done in my mind. Thank goodness for Longfellow and Shakespeare, whose poetry pulled me out of my nightly binge of unacceptance. There were so many more things I needed to accept in the months to come, and my husband not physically being there was just the first step. There were money issues, parenting issues, accepting that he was dating, and most of all, accepting that he stopped loving me the way I thought he always would. I also had to accept what I didn't see at the time and also accept all the things I didn't know when we were together. For me, acceptance is an ongoing process. I work continuously not to get stuck trying to undo what cannot be undone.

Try This Exercise: Let It Rain

The following exercise can help you cultivate more acceptance in your life, which can in turn lead to greater personal and professional success.

1. First, write down all the little stuff that annoys you each day, the stuff you can't control. I am talking about the traffic, your child's messy room, delays in an airport, or little comments a coworker makes that have nothing to do with your job. Recognize which things you cannot control and make a commitment right now to accept them. Yes, there will be surprises that come up each day, but if you create awareness around what's in your control and what's not, you will see how these little things create a bad mood, stress, or annoyance that can easily be released with a deep breath and a commitment to letting go of things that you can't control. The next time you get upset, remember to ask yourself, "Is this out of my control? Can I find peace instead?"

2. Problem acceptance can be more challenging because there are problems that we might be able to change moving forward. But when we start to feel angry, resistant, or sad, we still need to get into the habit of asking ourselves, "Can I change the fact that this situation is happening right now?" You might be able to change it in the next moment or tomorrow, but can you really change it right now? How would you feel if you accepted it? You can still feel pain even if you accept something, of course, but it's a pain that could evolve over time. You could stop caring about it, it could just mean less, or you could learn to live with it. Most of all, the situation can change. When you don't accept something, it's a

pain that might never go away. Remember, if you can't control something you want to change, it is like trying to stop the rain. If you have a problem, be thoughtful and process it. The sooner you accept it, the sooner you will be moving on to solutions. With the practice of problem acceptance, we become better at business. When you accept the problem, you will very quickly gain the clarity needed to become the first one in the room to solve the problem!

Chapter 3: September

Just Because Someone Says It, Doesn't Make It True

"Whenever you find yourself on the side of the majority,
it is time to pause and reflect."

—Mark Twain

* * *

SEPTEMBER came in harsh. My daughters were devastated, and experiencing their pain along with my own felt unbearable. My older daughter left for college, and my younger daughter and I were left to find a new way to live. I found many days and nights so difficult. I took sleeping aids at night and drank coffee all day long so as not to feel everything that was happening in the moment. This response might not seem so bad for some people, but for a kale-eating meditator like me, this was really taking a walk on the dark side. I worked at The Motherhood Center, tried to release a podcast each week, and went to bed as much as I could. I did have moments and days of clarity and peace when I would record my podcasts and do my spiritual practice, but part of that practice was filled with the pain I needed to process. I could not escape the prison of my pain without looking deep within my marriage and myself.

My husband and I texted minimally. There were some fights about the fact that he left and a few discussions about finances and the kids, but we had not spoken directly or dealt with anything of great magnitude. Out of nowhere, one day, a text from my husband said that he was trying to rent an apartment for himself that was expensive. I objected to it. I didn't think we could afford it, and I told him that he should stay at his sister's mostly vacant New York City apartment or get a studio apartment. His comfort was not at the top of my priority list. Affording our lives and paying the bills for now two apartments, school tuitions, and other expenses for the children definitely were. He responded to me with a very long text, defending his need for a nice apartment and—this was the zinger—explaining to me that the real reason he left me was because I was selfish.

It wasn't bad enough that he left without warning, broke my heart, broke my kids' hearts, and that I had begged him to stay. I had been willing to work on anything to save the relationship and to move forward, but now he was saying he'd left me because I was "selfish." After the breakup, I thought any new wave of pain could never feel as bad as the first. But this one did. I instantly began questioning myself because—as he well knew—that's what I do. Was I selfish? He had left me, and now he was giving me the gift of blaming myself!

Had I loved myself more in that moment, I would have seen that he was only looking to blame me for his own choice to leave, but as it was, I felt destroyed.

I started going every week to the therapist who had been our marriage counselor to understand how I might have been selfish (along with processing whether I had been wrong to tell the children he was leaving). I kept asking her what I did over and over again. Her reply was consistent. "You really didn't do anything, Allison. He wanted a new life. It had more to do with him than you."

Yet week after week, his words about my selfishness haunted me. I am not saying that I was perfect in my marriage. Like every married couple, we needed to work on things. There were things I needed to work on, but ultimately, he didn't want to work on our marriage. Still, I went through it all in my mind every day and every night, questioning myself, my behavior, and my motives over the years.

One of the most painful things anyone can say to a woman is that she is selfish. Many of us take pride in our nurturing and loving those around us. Like me, if you are also empathic, you may try to fix problems for people around you because you feel the world and others' pain so deeply. For better or worse, women worldwide often base our value and worth on how well we help people and how they react to us. I am no longer clear if these attributes long associated with womanhood—nurturers, fixers, and helpers—are innate or just the result of a world that doesn't truly welcome our power. Either way, I owned these characteristics as ones that define me, just like many women do around the world.

As women, one of the only ways we will become fully realized and truly successful in our relationships and the business world is to create a separate identity from others and cultivate self-love and self-trust. After my husband left me, I needed to work on all these things, and for me, it was the ultimate failure to be considered selfish. I obsessed day and night about how I might be selfish. I would list things about our marriage in bed at night. I was my husband's best friend. I took care of our children. I cooked his meals. I dealt with a lot of the finances. I looked after his health. I tried to help him with his business and every day listened to his problems. I earned money, although he did earn more. I didn't go out much without him. Where had I been selfish? What had I done to make him leave me? During this time, if I were lucky, I would fall asleep at 4:00 a.m.

As I tortured myself with these thoughts day after day, I was reminded of Jean, a former client of mine. Jean was married, in her late forties, and had children in high school. Her husband left her just before we started our work together. He also texted her a few weeks later, blaming her for why he left. At first, I thought to myself, *How can this be?* How was I living out my client's life? Was this karma? I was in such a low place that I even wondered—had I given her bad advice, and was it coming back to haunt me? I was so fragile and messy that I was afraid to track down what advice I had given Jean, but I was also desperate. I quickly went through my old notebooks. It took me a long time to find the notes from our meeting on this topic. I opened notebook after notebook until I found a red notebook at the bottom of my dresser drawer. I know most people keep clothes in dressers, but that is where I keep notes on my clients and my own writings. And, of course, my notes on Jean were in the last notebook I looked through. But there it was written in all caps. My response to Jean was this: "Just because he said it, doesn't mean it's true!"

Again, I felt like I was speaking in those notes to my future self. I took in the words, and they gave me comfort for a moment. But could I truly take my own advice?

In my experience, this tendency toward self-doubt based on others' opinions is definitely more prevalent among women than it is among men. The problem of instantly believing that whatever others say about us is true often slows us down, makes us doubt ourselves, or forces us to give up too soon. How we are brought up as women in this society has a lot to do with it, and it is reinforced by our experiences at work, especially when we see our male counterparts getting paid more, getting promoted more, or succeeding more. *What's wrong with us?* We start to question. *Something must be.*

Women have the opportunity to change this dynamic of self-doubt right now, but if we believe everything we are told without looking within ourselves, the dynamic can never change.

I have suffered from self-doubt based on others' perceptions throughout most of my life. I always fought hard for myself and my clients, but I was driven by my code of ethics and sense of "doing the right thing" for others, not a strong sense of identity or deep self-love. Whatever I faced, regardless of the outcome, I would doubt myself. I'd toss and turn, lacking clarity about my behavior. But the truth is that sometimes people will say things to us that are not true or, at the very least, not true for us.

Years ago, when I first set up my own law practice, I negotiated a corporate agreement for a client who owned a small architecture firm. She was entering into a contract with a larger company that was represented by an attorney who went to Harvard Law School. I came into the transaction with a bit of an inferiority complex because I was an Ivy League dropout. (I dropped out of Cornell University during my undergraduate years and, although I ended up graduating from a reputable law school, it was not on par with Harvard.)

In the middle of negotiating the contract, I strongly opposed a clause in the contract that I believed could hurt my client's right to payment in the future. The response of the company's attorney was, "No one's ever had a problem with that provision before." My quick comeback was, "There's always a first time for everything." He told me he'd look into it.

I knew in my heart that my client needed the protection I fought for, but when I got off the phone, I became extremely doubtful about my position because of what the Harvard attorney had said to me. I even wondered if he looked down upon me. I felt terrible about myself and, although I eventually won the point, I was emotionally exhausted. At that time, I could spend days beating myself up about the little and big things in every area of my life.

But now, reeling from my husband's accusation, I had no choice but to take a stand against self-doubt. I was at a crossroads. *Selfish.* If I believed my husband's words because he said them and I didn't question them, I would be blaming myself for the end of our marriage. And for what? He broke our wedding vows and our lifelong commitment to each other. He chose not to work on the marriage. He chose not to live with his children anymore. He chose another life other than the family life we had created together. Yes, I needed to understand what I had done wrong in our marriage to grow, but I also needed to embrace the mantra: *Just because someone says it, doesn't make it true.*

I needed to empower myself, understand what happened to our relationship from my own perspective, and figure out what I needed to know moving forward. Believe me, this mantra took a while to sink in. I went through my doubt process, contemplating what he said, but then one night at the end of September, at about 4:00 a.m. in the morning, I concluded something important. In the end, he left. It was his choice. He left because of him. Ultimately, realizing he'd left because of him and not me was one of my first acts of self-love regarding the end of my marriage.

That is what we are doing when we embrace this mantra. We are loving ourselves enough to question the world around us and committing to look within to find our ultimate truth.

***

Believe it or not, *just because someone says it, doesn't make it true* is one of the most important mantras in business for every woman, whether you are running your own business, pursuing a creative career, working as a professional, or building a career as an employee in corporate America. People can say all kinds of things to us about our looks, our intelligence, or even job prospects and performance, and sometimes these things can be hurtful. However, we need always to remember that others' words about us aren't always right. In order for us to figure out what we should believe and not believe, we need to find our own center and value ourselves enough to explore how we truly feel and what resonates for us. We must ignore the outside chatter to allow ourselves to find our own paths.

As I discussed in a previous chapter, my need for certainty drove me to become a tax attorney and eventually a business consultant/coach. I loved to look at a client's financial statement, bank statements, or balance sheet because numbers were "certain" and always told the truth. Now, what a business owner did with those financial figures was a choice, but I always knew that our conversations about their business were anchored in objective, not subjective, truth. The numbers always supported my thoughts and assertions to help people grow their businesses.

But we don't always have a financial statement or balance sheet for our personal relationships, business relationships, or how we see ourselves in the world. So, how do we manage what other people say to us? How do we manage what we believe is true about ourselves, and what is not true? My work as a business and life coach has shown me the way forward on this point. Over the years, I have seen a common denominator, especially with the female clients I've worked with. Too many have doubted their abilities to succeed profession- ally, especially when they are struggling with the expectations of par- ents, partners, children, and society as a whole. It all comes down to loving ourselves or not, and if we could wave a magic wand to fully embrace who we are, we wouldn't need books like this one. All of the lessons in this book are intended to help us love ourselves more as we live with uncertainty, gain acceptance, and work on believing what our own voice tells us. We need to believe ourselves more than we believe the voices outside of us when it comes to what we're good at and what we're not, what kind of people we are and who we're not, and what we can and cannot do.

How can we elevate our internal voice to manage our beliefs about what other people say to us? First, if we're not centered within ourselves, we will be significantly swayed by what other people tell us. This can happen in business or personal relationships. We may have a coworker who is acting against us or be in a relationship with someone who is telling us we're wrong all the time when we've done nothing wrong. Whether we believe people in the outside world or not depends on our relationship with our inside world. It is even more challenging to know if what someone says is true or not when we don't yet have clarity. Sometimes we need to wait. Whether we need to wait, whether the other person is right, or whether we still need to connect with our inner truth, the only way we're going to move forward is if we have a firm center within ourselves.

One of the most crucial aspects of creating a firm center is realizing that nobody in the world has more value than you do. Sometimes we think someone is more valuable or more important based on their position in a company or how they are perceived in society, but that's not true. Yes, there are people who are experts, and we can go to them for advice on a particular matter. But ultimately, we need to pave the way for our own lives, always reminding ourselves to say, "Just because someone else said it, doesn't make it true." We need to figure out what is true for ourselves, what works for us. If you are at a company where you feel you are not valued and can't succeed, maybe you need to improve your skills or work harder, but maybe the company is not aligned with your values, and it could be that you need to leave. When your inner voice becomes louder, you stop believing everything the outside world is showing you. Over time you will gain clarity as to where you need to go and what you need to do.

This goes for everything that people say to you in life. Just because someone thinks you're selfish, heavy, not good-looking, too old, not smart enough, or not the right person for the job, that doesn't mean there's something wrong with you. These outside judgments or events don't dictate your reality unless you believe them to be true. Again, the reason why we believe what other people say is because we think they know more than we do. The minute we realize that whatever people say might not be true, we are acting with love and respect toward ourselves. We may then center ourselves and decide if what they are saying feels right to us. Sometimes you know what they are saying is not true because of an experience you've had, and other times you're aware that certain facts aren't true because you read a study or you have expertise. More often, however, you know it's not true because it just doesn't align or feel right. By owning this mantra—*just because someone says it, doesn't make it true*—you respect and trust yourself enough as the source for answers in your own life.

Whether it's in business or private relationships, the only way to gain clarity is to take a step back. This process is not about automatically thinking the other person is wrong. You can think, *I'm going to consider what this person says to me. Maybe this person is telling me the truth, but I'm going to go back to my center. I'm going to breathe. I'm going to make sure I'm feeling okay about myself, and then I'm going to take another look at the situation.* It's really about finding our own wholeness and our own self-love, so that we can see what we believe is true in this lifetime.

Sometimes there is no single answer to a problem you face, and sometimes, in the end, people have two different opinions. No one's right and no one's wrong. The right way forward is what works for you. Everyone can tell you not to pass up that job because it's the best job in the world, but just because they say it doesn't make it true for you. Someone could tell you that a guy is great so you should go out with him, but if you don't like him, you shouldn't go out with him. Someone can tell you to wear that dress, not to wear those shoes, or to live here or there, but just because they say it doesn't make it true for you. The only way you're going to have a happy, beautiful, and authentic life is to believe in yourself and believe what you think is true.

We're not always going to know the right answer immediately, and we're going to have doubts, of course, and sometimes other people will actually give us great advice. It's a balance that we have to strike, but it's an essential one. But the closer you get to your center, the more you love yourself, and the more you get to know yourself, the better you'll know your own truth. Then, when someone says something to you, you will know how to react, and you will know what to do to live your best life.

I have no idea if my husband still thinks he left me because I was selfish, but for me, just because he said it, doesn't make it true. This idea saved me throughout the first year he left me, and it continues to help me today at board meetings, while watching the news, and dealing with my husband moving forward.

After his communication about wanting an expensive apartment and his calling me selfish when I resisted, we ended up compromising on an acceptable price for an apartment. But then I heard from my daughters that he blamed me for the fact that his cheaper apartment was too loud and not as nice as he wanted. When my girls told me this, I felt my heart start to flutter. Was I wrong to argue that he should pay less for an apartment because of our current financial situation? Was it my fault he took that exact apartment? Was I selfish? And then I quickly caught myself. He was responsible for how he left. He was responsible for leaving at a time when we had large financial responsibilities. He was on his own, making his own choices. He was responsible if he lived in an apartment that was noisy, and he was responsible for living in an apartment that he did not like. He was responsible for all of his actions and his thoughts. I was not selfish. Just because he said it, doesn't make it true.

Try This Exercise: Embrace the Mantra

The minute your boss, spouse, or friend says something that makes you feel bad, doubtful, or like what you want in your life is not possible, before you even let it penetrate your skin, say the mantra, "Just because they said it, doesn't make it true." Repeat it until you believe it.

Then, center yourself.

Ask yourself if patience is needed until you find your answer.

Whether you're able to do it through breathing, meditation, yoga, working out, or walking, you need some way to clear the outside world from your mind. When I center myself, I actually feel a ball of energy in the center of my chest. You might feel your center in your gut, you might feel it in your throat, but there's a place within you that you can focus your energy and feel balanced. Find it.

Now, ask yourself what is true for you. What aligns with your values, needs, and desires for your life? Stay close to you. What you want for your life is real. What others have to say, less so. Find your own truth and your path will reveal itself over time.

Chapter 4: October

Believe in Your Own Beauty

"The best and most beautiful things in life cannot be seen,
not touched, but are felt in the heart."

—Helen Keller

* * *

THE weekend before my husband put an end to marriage counseling, he had told me that we married each other too young and that he wanted to have experiences with other women. He then said to me, "This has nothing to do with how desirable you are." Needless to say, I instantly felt unlovable and unattractive. How could I not? He was going to the gym twice a day, admiring women who were at least twenty years younger than me. But his desire to "have experiences" with them had nothing to do with my age, my wrinkles, or my cellulite? According to him, I was still desirable, but he just wanted to try other items on the menu. I was thrown into a tailspin. I felt like I had been so naïve when meeting many of his business colleagues over the years. Many of them were on their second marriages with younger women. The stereotype that these men married their younger assistants from work or someone they met at the gym was all very real. My husband had always scoffed at these colleagues and made it seem as if we were different from all of those other couples, but now I faced a similar fate to all of those other first wives.

I had been so distraught about my family breaking up that I did not pay much attention to my looks or my body the first few months after my husband left. I was, quite frankly, just trying to survive. In early October, I got a call from a guy friend who said, "The best revenge is to look great, Allison. Eat well, work out, and do whatever you got to do to keep looking young."

This made me slightly sick to my stomach. "So, let me get this straight," I replied. "If I go to the gym every day and get some 'work' done on my face, I will be showing my husband that he's missed out?"

I kid you not, my friend said, "Yes!"

After I hung up, I started wondering. How is looking good the ultimate revenge for women? Plenty of people had been telling me I should be prepared to see my husband with a thirty-five-year-old woman who was looking to spend our money (in fact, she would turn out to be thirty-three!). I was also told that for me, the target age for a new boyfriend was between sixty and seventy years old. I have nothing against anyone of any age, but these "rules" struck me as very arcane. My heart sunk. Was this my new reality?

After this phone call, I felt very shaky. My mind was telling me to ignore my friend's advice, but my emotions were a mess. In an attempt to inflict "revenge" on my husband, I decided to go to a holistic ayurvedic spa and consult with a renowned beauty expert. I have always been into organic and natural ways of living, so of course, true to form, I was going to inflict "holistic organic revenge" on my husband!

I quickly made an appointment at Pratima Spa to meet the owner, Pratima Raichur, for a beauty consultation. The spa was in a hip building in Soho, and in the elevator I started to think, *Hey, this might really work.* As I sat in their waiting room surrounded by natural, age-defying serums, I began to look through their menu of treatments. I became excited to wipe away my wrinkles in ultimate holistic revenge. But as I sat down with Pratima, I immediately started to cry. I went from speaking about my wrinkles to spilling everything about my husband leaving me. It turns out Pratima was much more than a wrinkle expert. She was a very wise healer too. I do admit that she had the most beautiful skin I have ever seen, and I was in shock to learn that she was at least eighty years old. But we weren't talking about wrinkles. She explained to me that my husband and I had been on a journey and that it had come to an end. In order to feel and look good, I needed to accept the situation, forgive, love myself, and have gratitude. It would have been much easier to get a good moisturizer, but that was her sage advice. She did also send me home with some herbs, serums, and her book, *Absolute Beauty*.

My plan for holistic organic revenge was quickly fizzling, and I got into my bed and started reading her book. What immediately caught my eye was the definition of beauty that she pulled from the Merriam-Webster dictionary: "that which gives the highest degree of pleasure to the senses or the mind. . . ."[1] I sat and read this definition in her book over again and again. I actually said out loud, "What? Beauty is what gives *me* pleasure, not someone else?" (Today, Merriam-Webster's online dictionary defines beauty as "the quality or aggregate of qualities in a person or thing that gives pleasure to the senses or pleasurably exalts the mind or spirit."[2] The older definition in Pratima's book and this newer online definition both clearly provide the understanding that beauty is what gives each individual pleasure whether it be through their senses, mind or spirit.) I had spent my entire life dressing a certain way, plucking my eyebrows, and wearing makeup to conform to a conventional standard of beauty so that I would be accepted and liked by men in the workplace and beyond. But here, the Merriam-Webster dictionary was

---

1 Raichur, P., & Cohn, M. (1997). *Absolute Beauty*. New York: HarperCollins, page 6.

2 *Merriam-Webster Dictionary, s.v.* "beauty," accessed March 22, 2021, https://www.merriam-webster.com/dictionary/beauty.

saying that real beauty is what gives me pleasure. That had never crossed my mind.

*　*　*

I think many of us are aware of how the media crafts public and private attitudes about our physical bodies that are often negative. In most advertising campaigns, women's bodies are photoshopped at least twenty to thirty times, creating images of women with unrealistic body proportions, no wrinkles, and not a single pore on their face.[3] It could easily be argued that no woman could possibly look like so many of the advertisements or media images we are bombarded with every day. We know that we are being sold an unattainable vision of physical perfection, and we say we reject it, but deep down on some level how can we withstand the barrage? It's no wonder why 91 percent of women are unhappy with their bodies.[4]

Even yoga, which was always my go-to workout practice, is now often advertised as a means to achieve a toned body adorned in expensive workout wear. I love the new wave of advertisements that talk about self-love and true beauty, but have you ever noticed how most women in these ads look incredibly fit and perfect? And who the heck are running these advertising companies and corporations that are so bent on making women feel bad first so that *they* can help us feel better? Although there are more female-owned beauty businesses than ever before,[5] men still dominate the fifty-billion-dollar industry.[6] Unfortunately, this industry continues to push a "certain

---

3   Jhally, S. (Director, Editor), Kilbourne, J. (Editor) & Rabinovitz, D. (Cinematographer). (2010). *Killing Us Softly 4: Advertising's Image of Women* [Film]. Northampton, MA: Media Education Foundation.

4   Ibid.

5   American Express OPEN, (2018). *The 2018 State of Women-Owned Business Report*, 11.

6   Ledbetter, (2016). *Ledbetter Factsheet*, 7, https://ledbetter.medium.com/ledbetter-launches-to-spotlight-gender-in-leadership-at-the-worlds-biggest-brands-4288e3065ecf

look" for true beauty that misleads us into thinking it is the path that will help us get and keep a man!

And if that is not hard enough, women can be extremely challenged about their looks in the workplace as it relates to getting a job, a promotion, or making it to the C-suite. One can argue that handsome men use their looks to charm people and get ahead, but in my experience, men are often judged more on their competence than on their looks. Every woman who goes to work, or even leaves her home, knows on some level that she is being judged on how she looks. These judgments can be so harsh and unpredictable that even if we bought into the fact that women should look a certain way, there is not even a clear path as to how we should look to be successful in corporate America. Some studies suggest that women who take care of their appearance and conform to societal beauty norms earn more money.[7] While other studies suggest that attractive women are seen as less capable or less qualified for their positions.[8] There are also studies that indicate women who are perceived as more attractive may be rewarded for it earlier in their careers, but when they enter managerial positions, that changes.[9] These conflicting studies prove the inconsistency of how women are perceived and treated in the workplace.

In any case, being judged for our looks instead of our abilities makes us feel less than valuable, distracted, disempowered, controlled, and ultimately prevents us from getting ahead. Now, I am not saying that every woman feels this way, nor am I saying that every company discriminates against women for how they look. There is

7 Wong, J. and Penner, A. (2016). Gender and the returns to attractiveness, *Research in Social Stratification and Mobility, Volume 4*, 113–123, https://doi.org/10.1016/j.rssm.2016.04.002

8 Johnson, S., Sitzmann, T., and Nguyen, A. T. (2014). Don't hate me because I'm beautiful: Acknowledging appearance mitigates the "beauty is beastly" effect, *Organizational Behavior and Human Decision Processes, Volume 125* (2), 184–192, https://doi.org/10.1016/j.obhdp.2014.09.006

9 Heilman, M., and Stopeck, M. (1985). Being attractive, advantage or disadvantage? Performance-based evaluations and recommended personnel actions as a function of appearance, sex, and job type. *Organizational Behavior and Human Decision Processes, 35* (2), 202–215, https://doi.org/10.1016/0749-5978(85)90035-4

definitely more awareness and movement in a better direction as of late, but this issue cannot be ignored if we are trying to redefine our own beauty. Furthermore, I would be surprised if most women in corporate America have never been made to feel self-conscious about their looks by a coworker or a boss in a meeting or when they were "excluded from the boys' club."

When I was a young attorney, a colleague of mine always seemed to stare at my breasts. Today, there are stricter human resource policies and procedures in place to report incidents like this, but at that time, it was a hard thing to prove and there was no place to really report it. This colleague and I would be talking about revenue rulings by the Internal Revenue Service, depreciation of gas under the ground, and updates on the tax ramifications of certain new laws for public utilities, and at the same time, he would be staring at my chest. It made me uncomfortable. It distracted me. I felt vulnerable and not valued for my intelligence. Looking back, maybe I should have spoken to a partner, but instead, one day I very nicely said to my colleague, "Could you please stop staring at my breasts?" Of course, he immediately denied it. There is a chance that he didn't realize he was doing it, or I misinterpreted our interactions, but all I know is that after I said it, he never did it again! However, to protect his reputation, he told everyone in the department what I said and made a big joke about it. I had not told anybody other than my officemate what had happened, and now it was a big joke in the office. It made me feel so humiliated that I started wearing baggier and baggier shirts and jackets to work. I felt even more like I could never belong. I will never know why this colleague did what he did, but it was demeaning, and how he dealt with it afterward was very painful.

Until I worked at The Motherhood Center, I dealt with men in business for most of my career. I have heard jokes about men having a "work wife" who was always someone young and new in the office. I have seen men touch the backs of many young ladies and heard them talk about the looks of so many women in the office. I have heard inappropriate sexual jokes that degrade women, and I have seen pinups and pictures of naked women in men's offices and the occasional break room. I have also been touched on my face by an older colleague in the middle of a conversation when we were talking about a serious business matter. I asked him why he did it, and he said, "I wanted to see if your face felt as soft as it looked." Quite frankly, I didn't even know what to say, so I removed myself from the conversation as quickly as possible. Like many women, I was also once inappropriately touched, though for me it was not at work.

What is so crazy is that all of these men I just described also worked side by side with women who made no proven claims of harassment or discrimination. Some of these men seemed inclusive and caring at meetings. Some of them were good leaders at times, and many of them even called themselves feminists. I have no direct evidence that women were not promoted at these companies I worked for because of their gender, but more men were running the show. What I do know is that all of these incidents made me feel bad about how I looked, made me feel less than, and made me feel excluded and alienated in the business world. At times, I felt like I couldn't compete because of how I looked. Now I see it had more to do with the mere fact that I was a woman. Whether the men around me did it consciously or not, talking about women's looks and certain other behaviors were just a way to make me feel disempowered.

There is an entire world judging women on their outer beauty on some level. But here is the rub—yes, you are probably being judged, but you can't worry about it because you can't control it, and it is not the true source of your power or *your* pleasure. Do we need to keep fighting for new societal structures and new laws that promote fairness and inclusivity for all women? Of course! But in the meantime, if we can internally transcend these judgments, we are finally at a time in the United States and other countries around the world when women can find a way to be successful based on our true value. Sometimes not caring about how people think we look can help us gain more inner power.

When we don't understand our relationship with our beauty and how we may be held back, many of us give up in some way. We make ourselves small, shy away, or fail to speak up. Or we rely on our looks so much that we don't fully embrace our power, and deep down, we might not feel valuable. And as we age, if we rely on our looks too much, it can create instability and anxiety in our lives that is tough to fight. Whatever our reason, when we conform to what society asks of us in order to be accepted, we often give up on our dreams.

When the idea of beauty consumes us, we end up spending so many resources chasing this unattainable goal. We all know how much more time and money we have spent on our hair, makeup, nail polish, and moisturizers than most of our male business associates, husbands, or boyfriends just to look good enough to go to work, and often we make less than them. Imagine what we could do with all that extra time and money! Rejecting ourselves for how we look is often a major distraction from achieving what we truly want deep down in our hearts.

There is nothing wrong with enjoying clothes, makeup, or hair treatments. Some people approach all of this as an art, and it gives so many people pleasure. It is not the act itself, but the intention behind why we do all these things and ultimately how we truly feel about ourselves that matters. Beauty is the light that shines within, but we've misinterpreted it to be about how other people react to us.

I have also heard from some women who listened to my podcasts on beauty that they have surrendered this "mainstream" idea of beauty. They wear baggy clothes to work, they don't wear makeup, and they focus on their performance. While I think this is wonderful if it is authentic for them, I went through a period like this in my own life, but for all the wrong reasons. I was so tired of being judged that I hid my body from the world. I wore baggier clothes, as I did at the law firm early in my career, I wore my hair up, and I wore less makeup. But this was not who I was either. I wanted to escape the judgment, so I tried to make my femininity invisible. I often wondered if my struggle with being judged on my looks played a role in my husband's leaving. But I know now that he was always destined to leave as I aged.

The truth is that our search for beauty cannot come from a desire to be loved by others because then we will "fix" ourselves just to be loved. It must come from a love for ourselves, from a deep passion to see ourselves in our divine nature and perfection.

* * *

I felt so ugly when my husband left me. I felt so rejected that there was no blush, no cover-up, and no Botox that would give me a lift. I needed to redefine what beauty meant to me to see if beauty could become "that which gives pleasure to my senses or my mind," as Pratima suggested in her book. How could I feel whole as I walk out my door, go to work, and interact with the world without finding a way to embrace my true beauty?

I had nowhere else to turn. So, one day in October, I decided to explore beauty as that which was pleasurable to me and nobody else, just to see what would happen. I sat for a while, thinking about what gave me pleasure and what gave me pain. As I described, I was fully aware of the fact that the socially constructed idea of beauty was creating a lot of pain for me and not much pleasure. I started to question what my true beauty was. If I experienced my true beauty, how would I feel inside? I truly believed that I would feel pleasure and peace. I would feel whole. I would feel more freedom.

As I was playing with this idea, I decided to take a walk outside. It was a beautiful day, and it felt more like summer than fall. During my walk, I saw a young woman coming toward me. She was the picture of what I believed the media and mainstream culture would tell me is beauty. She had tanned skin, was blonde and skinny, and her toned, trim midriff was showing. I noticed that I thought to myself, almost below a conscious level, *Oh, that's how I should look. How come I don't look that way? How can I try to look that way?* I thought,

How will people ever like me? How will men be attracted to me? What if I don't measure up to that standard of beauty?

As this young woman approached, I noticed all of this running through my mind, but I managed to stop this train of thought. "What is the real definition of beauty?" I asked myself. The answer came: *that which gives pleasure to my senses or my mind.* When I looked at the woman through this lens, her image, while nice enough, gave me no more pleasure than I felt looking at the buildings all around me or the cars in the street. So, if her image gave me no particular pleasure, for me it was not the definition of beauty.

I am not saying that my husband or my brother or another man on the street might not look at her and feel pleasure from the way she looked, but it is not for us to tell someone else what beauty is for them. It is only our job to feel what beauty is for us. When I looked at this woman, I did not think ill of her or judge her, I just didn't feel any pleasure. For me, her blonde, fit, and tanned appearance didn't represent beauty. This realization was huge for me. I was able to recognize that what many people were telling me was beautiful, never resonated with me. It had never felt right for me. And once that awareness came to me, I was able to figure out what *was* beautiful to me, what mattered to me, and what made me feel whole.

Your image of what the media and mainstream culture tell you is beauty might be different than mine. But whatever our images might be, finding our own definitions of beauty could be a new measuring stick for all of us. If we can redefine our beauty based on what gives us pleasure, we are not fighting with the messaging from the outside world anymore. We have a new metric, and it is about our own senses. This connects us to how we truly feel. It has us asking ourselves the question, "What gives me pleasure?" And when you find your true definition of beauty, you will have less conflict inside of yourself. You will start to see your value differently. You will become whole, and this wholeness will generate a new light within you, a new place from which to manifest a new strength and power. And when you go out into the world with your authentic idea of beauty, you will attract things into your life that align with you.

Of course, we can still be rejected because of someone else's idea of beauty. But the point is that we won't be rejecting *ourselves*, as that, after all, is a form of the ultimate pain. We can leave a situation or a person, or they can leave us, but we can never get away from ourselves. It is very painful to live a life where our inner joy is dictated by something out of our control. And that's the thing. Nothing is permanent except one thing—the love we have for ourselves. The love we have for ourselves can last a lifetime. The love we have for ourselves can build our resilience as we give ourselves permission to have the most fabulous experiences because we aren't afraid. When we aren't afraid of showing up and accessing our unlimited potential, we are comfortable with who we are.

I know many people might be afraid to let go of all the things we need to do to be "beautiful" in our society—the hair, the makeup, the nails, the plastic surgery, etc.—and I am not saying that those things can't bring you legitimate pleasure. I am not saying you shouldn't do those things, and I am not saying that doing all of those things is not a true expression of yourself. I am just asking you to go back and define beauty *for yourself*, to align your definition with your senses, to align it with what you find pleasurable, and then go out into the world. You will experience so much less suffering and so much less self-rejection when you figure out what is pleasurable for you. And only you. Everyone has a different definition of beauty. Beauty really is in the eye of the beholder.

The minute we stop believing in society's definition of beauty, we gain more freedom. We think we need to look a certain way to get a guy or get a job, but all we need to do is empower ourselves and define our own idea of beauty. Once you empower yourself in every aspect of your life, you don't need a man to take care of you. You learn to take care of yourself at home and at work. Then, if you choose to have a relationship, it is based on your empowered choice. There is nothing more attractive than a woman who loves herself and

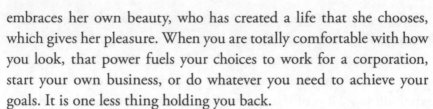

embraces her own beauty, who has created a life that she chooses, which gives her pleasure. When you are totally comfortable with how you look, that power fuels your choices to work for a corporation, start your own business, or do whatever you need to achieve your goals. It is one less thing holding you back.

Will you get less attention from men if you don't conform to a certain standard of beauty? Maybe. But who do you need to please in this lifetime? How will you live a fully realized life with internal peace, creativity, and self-love if you don't play by your own rules? And the best part is that when you see and express your own beauty, those who can see it too will be attracted to you and come into your life. You will be at peace to be your best self and be with others who recognize you. Living this way opens your heart and unleashes your creativity and strength, giving you the authentic power to pursue and achieve your goals. The absolute truth is that you are beautiful just the way you are and that when you see this, nothing can hold you back.

Before I shifted my understanding of beauty, whenever I felt ugly, judged, or not good enough because of my body, I entered every room without all my power. I felt less. I felt less in a business meeting, a board meeting, and on the beach with my family. I felt like I needed to compensate for what I was not and, by extension, my greatest assets and gifts were tainted and kept hidden. I elevated how I would be perceived physically as the marker of my value and success. In fact, when I would enter a business meeting or a social situation, how I looked was the first thing that was on my mind. It would take me several minutes to settle into where I was. I would use my humor and ability to make small talk to sink into the experience around me, forget my physical body, and engage with what was before me.

I have a long way to go in understanding beauty in terms of how I feel and what gives me pleasure, and not what others think is attractive. On this issue, I can only share with you what I have learned but not what I have mastered. Now, when I walk into a room, I have trained myself to say, "I am everything I need to be, I am whole, and I am not looking for anyone to validate me." I hope one day I won't even need to think about it, but for now, these few thoughts keep me aligned with accepting my body and my looks no matter where I go. It helps me realize that when I walk into a room, I am there to have an experience, share myself with others, and be open enough to receive what is before me. I still tell jokes and make small talk, but it is more natural and comfortable. Everyone has a different issue with why they are not empowered. For me, before this transformation, if you called me stupid I wouldn't have believed you. But if you called me ugly, it would have ruined my day. Now that I am experimenting with feeling my beauty from a different perspective, I feel freer to enter any room. Do I fall off the wagon while looking at Instagram or going to a party? Of course! But I have so many more moments when I truly feel my worth and my value like never before.

Owning our beauty as women is a key element to accessing our inner strength and preventing so many distractions and disempowering moments. It's not that we won't ever be judged for how we look, but we can stop judging ourselves for how we look and hold our power. I feel like I am in the process of doing this. I still wear makeup, high heels when it feels good, and I may buy an outfit to be more "in style," but I try to feel it all from my own senses. When I walk out the door in the morning, I commit to the idea that true beauty is what gives me pleasure.

Try This Exercise: Own Your True Beauty

1. Absorb a new definition of beauty: "That which gives pleasure to your senses or your mind." Think about the belief system that gives you pain and list beliefs or practices you'd like to shed. Then, list things that give you pleasure. Begin to surround yourself with these things.
2. Dressing rooms are tough! Even with my new definition of beauty, I can still get sidetracked sometimes by the "standard

of beauty" when I go into a store and the clothes don't fit or I don't like how I look. My mind can start going to a bad place. But then I look in the mirror and start thinking about the purpose of my body, which helps me realize my life's purpose. I actually stand there in the dressing room sometimes and I look at my legs and say, "Walking legs. These are my legs that help me walk and move and go where I need to go." I look at my arms and say, "Doing arms. These arms help me write and drive and eat. They are beloved by me." I look at my eyes, nose, and mouth and name their function. I start to feel my beauty, and a beautiful peace comes over me. It also sometimes helps me find something I like to wear, a form that complements the function I am celebrating!

3. Pull away a little bit from the obsession with your physical body. Spend more time thinking about what makes you unique, what makes you special, and what you like and what you don't. Start creating your own definition of what beauty is to you and hold these ideas throughout the day. If you find yourself getting upset while you are out at a bar, with friends, or in a meeting at work, pull back from what you think others are thinking. Feel your own awareness and true nature. Try to become aware of what gives you pleasure. Know that you have a right to be in the place you are in and that there is nothing wrong with you. There never has been anything wrong with you and never will be. Let your light shine beyond the situation you are in and appreciate your own true beauty. You can also use my mantra when you walk into any room: "I am everything I need to be, I am whole, and I am not looking for anyone to validate me."

Discovering your own beauty helps you depend on yourself, and not another person, to live your life. That is real safety, real value, and can only lead to real happiness, real success, and more true beauty in your life!

Chapter 5: November
There Is Only One Person You Need to Trust

"Trust thyself: every heart vibrates to that iron string."

—Ralph Waldo Emerson

* * *

As the seasons changed and the weather became colder, it began to hit me that my separation from my husband was becoming more permanent. I was still in pain, but I began making plans with friends and finding more things to do with my free time. I quickly learned that quality and not quantity was the better way to go when it came to socializing in my current state.

One night, I made plans with a woman I did not know that well. She was not a close friend and did not know much about my life or my devolved marriage, but she was single, and I was trying to make new connections in my life. We met in a little café in the East Village. It was so dimly lit that I could barely see the menu, but I was not going to complain. I was out, I was pushing forward, and I was making a new friendship. After we ordered drinks, my new friend said to me, "You know your husband cheated on you, right? No man just leaves without having someone else in his back pocket." I literally felt as if I'd been stabbed in my stomach. It had never occurred to me that my husband might have cheated on me. I had trusted him with my life. As I entertained the possibility that she was right, I realized that I had separated that piece—my trust in him—from the situation. I think I had been saying to myself that, yes, he'd left, but I could still trust him in the big picture.

I finished my meal in a state of shock and excused myself. I was not mad at this woman. In fact, I remembered that when my husband told me he wanted to separate, I felt a split in my heart. In that moment, all my anger and grievances toward everyone other than my husband went away. I couldn't even muster up any emotion toward this woman now, although I knew we would never meet again. My heart just could not take it.

As I lay awake in bed that night, I thought back to all the things my husband might not have told me. To blurt out on June 30 that he was leaving must have taken some forethought. He obviously had a plan to leave. We'd had dinners, conversations, and shared so many intimate moments in the months leading up to that day. For how long had he been planning on leaving me? The next day I made an emergency appointment and ran to my therapist to resolve this fear and this pain. She had been our marriage counselor, and I knew my husband had also seen her a few times after leaving me. Would she know the answer? If she did, she probably couldn't tell me anyway. And what if he'd never revealed anything like that to her? People only let us know what they want us to know. Why was he in such a rush to leave? Why wouldn't he stay in counseling? What was he running toward?

The therapist didn't know anything more than I did. However, after my appointment, I learned one thing for sure—that asking questions you will most likely never know the answer to leads to unbearable suffering. And at this point, it didn't matter what happened before he left. He was gone, and I had to continue to find a way to move forward. I finally asked myself the most relevant question: "How can I ever trust anyone again?" It felt like such an out-of-control question. Clearly, I was looking outside of myself for something to make me feel safe and secure. But I was only left with me. Sure, I had family and friends who had stood by my side, but every night I was alone in the darkness. After a week of not sleeping, I heard the answer loud and clear. The only person I truly needed to trust was . . . me. A strange feeling of relief washed over me. I am not saying that I never planned to trust anyone else in my life; I was just finally seeing that my priority had to be trusting myself.

When you don't trust yourself, you may feel things but don't often act on them. When you don't trust yourself, you don't start a new business, apply for a new job, or speak your mind at work because you are afraid you are wrong or can't achieve what you want. In everything we say, we are targets, allowing the world to make us feel wrong. And if we are working and competing against men in any industry, trusting ourselves is one of the most essential qualities to get ahead.

One of the most challenging times for women is when they first enter the workplace,[10] and I had found this to be true myself. Women don't have work experience to rely on, so we are more vulnerable to inequities in the workplace. It is not that as we move forward and get promotions, our level of equality with our male counterparts rises, but over time our work experience gives us some expertise to lean on, even if we never achieve perfect equality. As I stated in the introduction to this book, a recent study shows that even though men and women enter the workforce at equal rates,[11] men are two times more likely to get promoted in the first five years of working,[12] and this doesn't even touch upon how women are harassed, mistreated, excluded, or not listened to in so many situations in the workplace.

---

10 Vanessa Fuhrmans, "Where Women Fall Behind at Work," *The Wall Street Journal*, 15 Oct 2019, https://www.wsj.com/articles/where-women-fall-behind-at-work-the-first-step-into-management-11571112361

11 LeanIn.Org & McKinsey, (2018). *Women in the Workplace, McKinsey & Company*, 6.

12 LeanIn.Org & McKinsey, (2018). *Women in the Workplace, McKinsey & Company*, 8.

When we are faced with these challenges, we often lose trust that we will find our way when the odds are stacked against us.

I had this experience in my first job as a tax attorney at a large law firm. I was definitely ignored more by certain partners than some of my male colleagues were, and the head of the department often called me by the wrong name—Anne, the woman he had fired in my department right before I got to the firm. But I also felt like I was passed over for a good opportunity when a fellow attorney who started at the same time as me was moved to another department with a bigger connection to revenue at the firm. He and another attorney, who was senior to me, later launched very successful careers as a result of joining this department. They both were very smart and well-deserving, but so was I, and I didn't even get a chance to do any work for that department to prove myself. I was often given state tax law assignments, and I had minimal contact with clients. I can't prove to anyone why it happened, but both men moving to that department got a type of promotion in my eyes. I remember wondering what I did wrong. I felt shorted, like there was limited opportunity for me to move forward at the firm. It made me feel uncertain about my future and whether I would find success. At that point in my life, I did not trust that I would be okay no matter what.

Although I could be wobbly on my self-trust, I completely trusted my husband. When it came to personal business matters, I was a bit more cautious, but I essentially took people at their word until they broke a promise. In my roles as a lawyer and a business consultant, I met people who did not trust anyone. One of the most challenging clients I ever had was a woman business owner who always told me, "Allison, the only way to be good at business is to trust nobody." She didn't trust the people who worked for her. She didn't trust her clients. In business, you need to protect yourself in your contracts and be prepared for broken promises, but you also need to be practical. No matter the contract's final language, you need to have trust to a certain extent and take some risks in your business dealings to be successful.

Sure, a few of her clients did break contracts, but that is just the nature of doing business. Most of her clients honored the terms of their agreements. However, she did lose several clients over the years because she failed to create strong relationships with them. There were some disappointing employees, but many more excellent ones ended up leaving because of her behavior. In never trusting anybody, she placed a shield between herself and the rest of the world.

Years later, I understand that if this client had more trust in herself, she probably would have had more room to create better relationships in her business life. She could have taken more risks and discovered more possibilities. She would have believed that if she had a problem, she could figure it out. Sure, she could have trusted other people more, too, but the real point is that trusting yourself gives you the courage to live your best life, which includes interacting with others in a healthy way.

We spend too much time fearing the pain and heartache that we might suffer if someone breaks our trust. It's not that we don't have to be aware of the people that we're dealing with because sometimes it's obvious that we shouldn't be involved with a particular person. Other times, though, we can never foresee how someone will mistreat us, betray us, or break a contract. But as I learned this year, we can survive so much pain in our lives and always find our way back home if we trust ourselves on our life's journey.

* * *

I think all of us understand what it's like for someone to break our trust and how hard it is to rebound. Over the course of this year, it has become evident to me that the problem is this: if we spend our lives not trusting people because of things that happened in the past, our hearts won't be open when something happens to us that we *can* trust. We need to be intimate and enjoy special encounters with the human race. Without trust in ourselves, we won't get close to anyone, whether a coworker or someone new in our lives. We won't have profound relationships. We will also fail to take acceptable business risks and be our most creative selves because protecting ourselves will be more important than creating a life that represents our desires, goals, and individuality. Without self-trust, we will keep pulling away from the world because we assume everybody's horrible and untrustworthy. Our hearts won't be open enough to take advantage of the experiences that are right in front of us.

The truth is that all of us are going to get hurt in our personal and business lives. We are going to have people leave us, lie to us, and disappoint us. We are going to lose jobs and contracts and have people break their promises and break our hearts when they give a business opportunity to someone else. People in our lives will blame us for their problems or say something that leaves us disappointed and breathless. It might all sound so terrible, but there is also so much joy in life. There are so many beautiful experiences that come not only from triumphs but also out of pain. The relationships that last, the businesses we start, and the new things we create all spring from trust. There is so much depth to life, and without self-trust, it will be hard to enjoy these new experiences.

The most important thing is not to let any particular experience of "being burned" shut us down. If we look only for certainty in human relationships, we're going to shut down. If we live in the past, we're going to shut down. If we don't trust ourselves, we will think that whatever is to come will knock us out. But if you trust yourself, you're not thinking about what's coming because you know that whatever happens, you will figure it out, and that's the best way to live. If we trust ourselves and meet someone we can't trust, we'll figure it out. And if we trust ourselves and make a wrong business decision, we can also figure that out and still be okay.

I've also found that if you trust yourself, you will naturally be more centered, more openhearted, and more intuitive. You'll see things more for what they are, and you will make better decisions. You will attract better people in your life, and you'll attract better opportunities.

When we start to trust ourselves truly, we will gain the strength and the know-how, and the ability to weather any storm. That's ultimately what we want. Remember, gaining certainty in our lives is limited. We've already lived out the past, and we want certainty because we don't always trust ourselves to be resilient in this moment and the future. But when we trust ourselves, we don't need to know all the answers. Life becomes more exciting because we know new things are always going to come into our lives. We just need to show up for them and do the best we can. All of us have this innate ability to live our best lives. This mindset will lead us to new opportunities, help us discover new ideas, and help us meet new people. It's possible for all of us. We just need to create a strong, trusting relationship with ourselves.

The world can break our hearts repeatedly, but if we trust ourselves, we will keep getting up and experiencing life, and our path will keep unfolding. I promise you, you will find success. You will find love, and you will find friendship. Most importantly, you will find wholeness. And all you need to do is know that the person you are is enough. Trust that person, trust that inner voice, and trust your path because you are already everything you need to be. You do not need anybody else in your life to tell you that!

Looking back, I trusted myself in business and my personal life in so many ways, but fundamentally I relied on my husband to be okay. Although I believed in this concept of self-trust (and even taught it!), I didn't realize that I wasn't fully living it until I was left alone. I trusted myself up to a point, but I didn't fully engage in the world around me with freedom and a deep understanding of all that I was capable of. I think many other women have the same problem. We fail to see that the limits on our opportunities often have nothing to do with our capabilities. We end up looking for safety by trusting our jobs, our spouses, and our friends more than the voice within us because if we really were so great, why would there be so many obstacles? If we really were so great, why wouldn't we have more success? But many of the obstacles we face in the business world, and even in our personal lives, were created long before we arrived. We need an unwavering trust in ourselves to help us navigate the bumpy road of being a woman in this world so that we don't give up on ourselves or our dreams.

For me, the implications of self-trust now extend far beyond the business world. The only way to keep my heart open is to trust myself fully. If not, I will not be able to move on because I will spend my life playing it safe, mistrusting others, and most of all, mistrusting the life I was meant to live. Who knows, maybe one day I will even muster up enough self-trust to fall in love again. In the meantime, I am building trust in myself.

Try This Exercise: You Trust You

How do we trust ourselves and turn down the volume on the outside world? We do this by turning down the volume on our past and turning down the volume on our future. We center ourselves in this moment, and we breathe to connect with our deepest selves. And then we ask ourselves, "What are my goals? What are my passions? What's holding me back?" and "If I trust in myself right now, what will I do?"

Remember that from birth to death, you only have you. You will always be with yourself. It's funny. We try to count on other people, but we're the only person we will always be with, so we have to learn to rely on ourselves. We have no choice but to trust ourselves. We can spend our whole lives trying to get other people to give us the answers when all along the answers are within us. We cultivate self-trust by living, listening to our inner voice, honoring our thoughts, and knowing that the outside world is just noise.

We don't want to shut our hearts down because our hearts lead us to the places we need to go and the people we need to meet. Life is not about avoiding being hurt or making the safest decisions. Life is about living our best lives.

Say at least a few times a day to yourself, "I trust that no matter what happens, I will be okay. I trust myself."

Chapter 6: December and January
Everyone Suffers:
Don't Let It Stop You

"We must learn to endure what we cannot avoid. Our life is composed, like the harmony of the world, of contrary things, also of different tones, sweet and harsh, sharp and flat, soft and loud. If a musician liked only one kind, what would he have to say?"

—Michel de Montaigne

* * *

DECEMBER and January of my year without men are forever joined together. These two long months were all about coming to a deeper understanding of suffering and the healing powers of the women in my life.

I was sitting with Dr. Birndorf one day in her office, and she asked me out of the blue about the last time I had a checkup. I guess she was thinking my body had been under extreme duress for almost six months, and it would be a good idea to go to the doctor. Just as in other realms of my life, I had recently switched my primary care physician from a male doctor to a female internist, Dr. Meredith Lash. She had been recommended to me by a friend.

On Dr. Birndorf's advice, I went to Dr. Lash for some blood work, and the minute she walked in, I started to cry. I told her that my husband had left me. This was not unusual for me during this time. Truth be told, whoever you were, if you spoke to me for more than ten minutes, even if you'd just met me, I might have spilled my story to you, too!

The doctor's initial response was to say she was very sorry. And then she asked me, "Were you happy with him?" That thought had never crossed my mind. It was as if she were asking me if I was happy with air or water. My family had been my sacred world, and it was the most important thing in my life. Had I been happy with him? I didn't know I even had the right to ask myself that question.

My husband and I had been best friends, I thought. We had taken a vow to work through anything and hold our family together. I never knew until the day he announced he wanted to separate that he didn't feel the same way I did about the world we had created. Was that happiness?

Dr. Lash started to examine me. She began the breast exam and paused over something in my left breast, probing, "Did you know about this lump?"

Panic rose in my throat. I said no, I had not noticed it. She quickly responded that she didn't think it was anything but that I should make an appointment for a mammogram. Fear and panic overcame me.

I left her office and immediately called the radiologist's office. The radiologist was another woman doctor I had switched to a few years earlier. Dr. Barbara Edelstein, like Dr. Lash, was another brilliant woman who had the ability to make you feel very safe and taken care of. When I told the receptionist about the lump, she responded that I hadn't been for a mammogram in three years. Considering my mother had breast cancer and so many of my friends, I felt it had been careless of me not to go earlier.

I felt so nervous and full of guilt that I actually began arguing with the receptionist that I *had* been in for a mammogram within the last three years. Finally, the woman said, "We can keep arguing this point, or I can fit you in tomorrow morning at 8:30." It was like a jolt back to reality. I gratefully accepted the appointment.

The next day at Dr. Edelstein's office, I immediately showed her the lump. She didn't think it was anything, but she sent me into the mammogram room. After the mammogram, they took a sonogram, and I noticed that Dr. Edelstein got very quiet. Again, I started to panic, but this time I thought, *Maybe everything is okay* again and again. When I went back into her office, she sat down and, looking me straight in the eyes, said, "You have some irregular tissue, Allison. You need to get a biopsy." I started to cry. I told her that my husband had left me.

The most challenging part of this situation with my breast was that I was acutely aware I was alone. The main person I was used to leaning on physically and emotionally was gone. I was not used to leaning on just myself or my friends. As I started to cry, I walked myself to the front of the office to make the appointment for my biopsy. I kept trying to recite "maybe" under my breath, but I felt my heart beating outside my chest. I heard what the woman making the appointment was saying to me, but I felt very removed at the same time. I left the office, and I called my best friend Robin, then I called my sister. I knew I needed to stay in maybe, but I was still in shock from my husband leaving me, and I felt that it was all too much to bear. I wasn't even thinking about myself. I was worried that my children needed me. I needed to be well for them.

In the wake of this news, women from all parts of my life gathered around me. I had more offers to take me to my biopsy than all the rejections I got from publishers for my first book! The lucky winner was my dear friend, Kate Walbert, a genius and accomplished writer, but most of all, a wonderful friend. I remember lying on the table during the biopsy feeling very cold, lonely, and praying that I would be okay. As I started to cry, the technician became worried that they were hurting me, and that the local anesthesia was not working. But these tears came from the pain in my heart. True

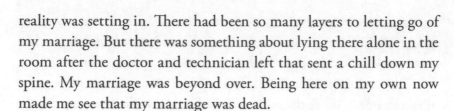

reality was setting in. There had been so many layers to letting go of my marriage. But there was something about lying there alone in the room after the doctor and technician left that sent a chill down my spine. My marriage was beyond over. Being here on my own now made me see that my marriage was dead.

I got the news of my biopsy a week later. The result was a papilloma that needed to be removed. But it was not cancer, they told me. I felt relieved! After a few weeks, I met another mighty woman named Dr. Elisa Port, who would be my breast surgeon. Dr. Port also had a deep confidence and strength that I had seen in the other two women doctors. The way she greeted me, the way she spoke, and how self-assured she was that she could help me were incredible. And, you guessed it, after a few minutes into my appointment, I started to cry and told her that my husband had left me. Just like the other female doctors, I loved their strength, and at the same time, their compassion and openness to discuss my personal situation with me. Dr. Port then turned to me and said, "I have some unfortunate news for you. They biopsied the wrong spot. They did find a papilloma, which is good, but it's not the spot that the radiologist was concerned about, so you need another biopsy."

Within a matter of three hours, I went from being totally relieved and happy that I was only going to have a minor surgery to the familiar intense uncertainty of whether or not I had breast cancer. They did the biopsy immediately at her facility, and this time, I was really by myself. I tried to call some friends from the waiting room, but nobody picked up. To make matters more painful, this biopsy was taken while my breast was in a mammogram machine. Although I was grateful for having good health care, in that moment I thought, *Isn't there another way to do this*? I left the hospital bandaged and in pain and once again worried about what my results would be. It was pretty incredible that I was only taken care of by women throughout this entire ordeal, including both biopsies. As time went on, it made me feel supported and not so alone.

I realized that there was something about working at The Motherhood Center that made me feel taken care of, too. They were beyond supportive about my surgery but also supportive about everything I was going through. I truly felt united in the mission with everyone that worked there, and there was no way to achieve the mission without working together. Looking back, I am certain that had any of the partners at my first job ever reached out to me, acknowledged me, and mentored me, I wouldn't have left after two and a half years. I felt that there was no path for me there because nobody was willing to walk beside me and help show me the way. I was willing to work so hard, stay late, and come in on weekends, but the culture didn't want me. They said they did (when I quit), but my experience at the firm demonstrated that I would never entirely be accepted in this environment, and I felt alone.

As my health scare continued, the atmosphere now surrounding me all felt so different. All of the women doctors, the women at The Motherhood Center, and my women friends and family gathered so close. I was suffering, but I was not alone.

* * *

After two days of waiting, I got a call from the doctor to discuss my biopsy. "I have good news," she said. The biopsy did not show cancer. But, she said, I had atypical cells, and atypical cells could mean something else. These cells could reside in a place where there is cancerous tissue. "So, you need to get it taken out." She went on to say that there was a high probability that it was nothing, but she could not rule out cancer without removing the tissue.

All of a sudden, my head started to spin. I wanted this to be over. I didn't want to be sick. I didn't want to have uncertainty. I didn't want *not* to know. I just wanted to go on with my life, but that's not what was happening. The doctor also told me that she was booking surgeries for the second week in January, and it would take a week to get the full biopsy back. Then, Dr. Port said, "Don't worry. Whatever this is, we will take care of it. I will help you through it." Now, I don't know about you, but I had never heard a doctor say something like this. I began to feel a little better.

My daughters wanted to come to the surgery with me, but I didn't want them to worry, so my sister came with me. It was nice to have her love and support. As I checked in, the receptionist looked over my paperwork. "Is this still your emergency contact?" she asked, reciting my husband's name and cell phone number. I blinked. I had given birth to our older daughter at this hospital, and they had all of my information from then, like some kind of time capsule.

I shook my head no. Because my information had changed, I had to fill out a new form, and I placed my sister as my emergency contact. At that moment, I wondered if someone had told me nineteen years earlier that I would be back at this hospital, separated from my husband, and getting breast surgery, I would have thought it was the most insane thing I ever heard. But here I was. Again, I felt a twinge in my heart, but life was moving forward, and I needed to be thankful for all the support I did have.

Soon after, I was taken to a room to prepare for surgery, and Dr. Port walked in and sat beside me. This time, she took my hand and again said these words, "Don't worry. Whatever this is, we will take care of it. I will help you through it." I might not have had a husband, but I had the most kick-ass woman doctor I had ever met telling me everything would be okay in the most reassuring and compassionate way. After the surgery, there was more wait time, but weeks later, I was given an appointment to see Dr. Port to discuss the results.

On the day of my appointment, I got to the hospital early, and my kick-ass mighty female doctor was in surgery, so I had to wait. Like most people waiting for results, I experienced the next sixty minutes as the longest of my life. And as I sat there looking around the waiting room, I took in the scene. There were numerous women with no hair. I saw older women and younger women all waiting for treatment or some news. Then, all of a sudden, a woman in a wheelchair was placed next to me in the waiting room by a nurse. I sat looking at this woman in the wheelchair. She looked like she was in her seventies. Half of her head was missing hair, her legs looked very swollen, and she seemed like she was in a daze. I wondered about her suffering. I wondered if she had breast cancer. I wondered if she had any other illness. I wondered how sick she was. And then I thought to myself, *Did I have a right to be suffering so much when my situation was probably not as dire?* I was sitting in this waiting room. I was strong. I was relatively healthy. Even if something were to be wrong with my body, it seemed like something that I could get through quickly. Then, I thought about a quote by Viktor Frankl that I had read many years ago.

For those of you who don't know of Viktor Frankl, he was an Austrian neurologist, psychiatrist, and holocaust survivor. In his bestselling book, *Man's Search for Meaning*, he chronicles his experiences in a concentration camp, which led him to discover the importance of finding meaning in all forms of existing, even the most brutal ones, to give us a reason to continue living. In his book, when he talked about suffering, he made an analogy. Frankl said, "A man's suffering is similar to the behavior of a gas. If a certain quantity of gas is pumped into an empty chamber, it will fill the chamber completely and evenly, no matter how big the chamber. Thus suffering completely fills the human soul and conscious mind, no matter whether the suffering is great or little. Therefore the 'size' of human suffering is absolutely relative."

In that moment, I realized that, however bad or good my situation, I was suffering. It seemed like this woman next to me was suffering. And there was no need to compare our suffering.

We're all going to experience suffering in our lives whether it comes to our health or a problem with a job, our children, or our partner. We tend to minimize suffering because we feel like we don't have a right to suffer or because others clearly suffer more. But when something upsets you, if it is like a gas that fills up a room, you have to acknowledge this suffering before you can move forward. Interestingly, Viktor Frankl also said that his time in a concentration

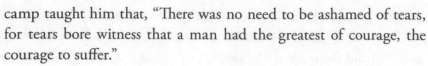

camp taught him that, "There was no need to be ashamed of tears, for tears bore witness that a man had the greatest of courage, the courage to suffer."

I realized in that moment that just because I was suffering, it didn't mean I wasn't courageous. My tears were not my weakness. My fear was not fragility. I was scared. I was human. Though I was holding out hope for many different possibilities, I still had tears and I still had worry.

I sat up a little taller in that waiting room. I felt my own courageousness. I realized that I didn't know what was going to happen, but I would have to handle it. Even feeling hopeful, I still bore the suffering of the situation, and there was something courageous about that. There was something brave about everybody who was sitting in that waiting room, willing to face whether they were sick or whether they were well. They were all willing to face their treatment, body scans, or their PET scans, and it didn't really matter who was suffering more or who was suffering less. It was more about how we show up for our own suffering.

All of this also made me think about my friend whose husband works as a cancer doctor in a hospital. When she's upset about something, he always turns around and says, "Well, at least you don't have cancer." He says this out of love because he's trying to offer her perspective, and it's understandable because a good perspective is very helpful. But before we attain perspective, we need to go back and acknowledge our suffering. Whether it's unreasonable to somebody else, silly, or indulgent, our suffering is our suffering. Sometimes it just fills up the room, whatever room we're in. Yes, you can consider different perspectives. But in that moment, it is often best to examine our suffering first, because only when we recognize the level of our own pain can we look for tools to alleviate it.

So, as I sat there and worried about my results, I allowed myself to suffer. I felt all my nervousness and fear. After about ten minutes, I decided to count my blessings. I acknowledged the fact that at that moment I felt healthy, I had beautiful blessings in my life, and I had beautiful things to look forward to. I did my maybe state-ments, (Maybe everything was okay. Maybe I would get better.) I did my breathing. I practiced acceptance. I had plenty of time to run through my toolbox. I was sitting there waiting for my appointment for almost an hour! And as I did all these things, I felt like I'd opened a window. It felt like the gas, my suffering, found a place to go and, in passing, more space was created within me.

Finally, my name was called. I walked into the office, and then the nurse came. Gently, she took off my bandages. She told me that I could resume activities the next day and asked me if I had any questions. Of course, my first question was, "What did my pathol-ogy say?" She smiled and said, "You can take a breath. Everything is okay." I quickly gave her a hug.

The surgeon came in, and we discussed the results. Everything was benign. She said my risk of breast cancer with atypia cells was higher than other women but not significantly higher. Then, she said, "Allison, you're free to go home and not come back." The first thing I did when I left that office was walk across the street to Central Park. I just wanted to be close to the grass. I wanted to be near a tree. I wanted to hear a bird. I wanted to feel close to the Earth. I also called my mother. It's so interesting when suffering leaves us. We feel the air. We feel relief. And we feel the glory of life and the depth of its meaning.

* * *

I know that everyone reading this book has had suffering in their life. As I have already discussed, there are many things we can't control in this lifetime, a lot of which can create suffering. We all have dif-ferent levels of suffering and we respond to our suffering in different ways. There is no point in judging or comparing your suffering to someone else's. If it fills up your mind like gas, this is how you are suffering. Similar to what Viktor Frankl said, there is no need to be ashamed of your tears, fears, anxieties, or worries, for these emotions bear witness to your courage, "the greatest of courage, the courage to suffer."

It also helps to realize that most of the time the suffering you are feeling is not unique to you. I have so many clients who come to me and tell me about how stressed they are or how overworked they feel, and that when they look around the office, they think that everybody else is okay. They believe that everybody else is balanced and that everybody else is doing a good job, but they are the only ones who can't handle it. What I have learned in my twenty-seven years in the business world is that, yes, sometimes there's somebody who's more sensitive than everybody else in the room. But if you're feeling overworked, there's a good chance that your male coworker next to you is feeling overworked, too, and so is the female coworker down the hall. Although this doesn't change the suffering of being overworked, it does allow you to see that you're not the only one.

There is something about believing you're the only one who's suffering that makes it worse. It's almost as if we turn the suffering on ourselves. We think we're not good enough. We believe that we're not capable. We may start to believe that there's something so weak inside of us because we are alone in suffering from a problem. In my experience, as women, we tend to feel worse about ourselves when we are suffering. We often feel like whatever is going on is about us not being able to handle a situation or not being strong enough instead of seeing the reality: that the situation in front of us is objectively difficult, and others would find it hard too.

When unexpected or challenging things happen in our lives, it can be shocking, disturbing, or upsetting. We might not be able to find our footing the moment the shock happens, but we can't judge ourselves for that. We can't judge ourselves for our suffering. As Viktor Frankl said, suffering just fills up the chamber. That's just what happens. Yes, we have a choice about what we're going to do with our suffering. Just like I did in the waiting room, we can open a window by shifting perspective. But in responding, we must be loving and kind to ourselves.

Even when I was going through the scare with my breast, I felt supported by my friends and family, who told me about similar experiences and how they had suffered. Some friends told me they also had a biopsy or that a friend of theirs had two biopsies or a lumpectomy, and others told me stories about people with breast cancer who survived. All of this helped. It helps us to know that whatever we're suffering from, we're most likely not the first person to suffer from it. Whether it's anxiety or depression or a problem with our children, there's something comforting about knowing that these problems exist in the world, that our suffering is, in a way, universal. It reminds us that just because we're suffering doesn't mean that there's something wrong with us.

* * *

Another aspect of accepting our suffering is realizing that life has suffering in it. I once believed that I was going to get to a point in my life when I would have no more suffering. I thought that all my fears and worries existed because I hadn't accomplished what I wanted to in my life. I believed that when I became an attorney and got that great job, I was going to have no more suffering. That didn't happen.

I've come to realize that just because there is suffering doesn't mean there can't also be happiness in your life. I think I believed that one day everything would just be okay. However, now I understand that even if your work life is prosperous, you can still have a relationship struggle with your partner. I understand that even if you are in good health, your client can still fire you next week. Life is complicated, but the good news is that it keeps changing. This is why techniques like maybe, gratitude, and acceptance can help shift our perspective and widen our view to include all that is good in our lives too.

We can't live our lives running from suffering because if we're so afraid of suffering, we won't make the choices that we want in our lives. We won't live our best lives because we'll always be trying to protect something. As much as you want to protect everything in your life, often the thing you least expect knocks you off your feet. I worried about so many things my entire life, but other than putting that one sentence in my book so many years ago, it never occurred to me that my husband would ever leave me. What I have learned this year is that just because you get knocked off your feet and you're suffering, it doesn't mean there can't be joy at the same time or that life won't change and even get better.

It's very understandable that sometimes our suffering takes over and becomes very overwhelming. But sometimes life is offering us something else, and we can't always see it. I am in no way minimizing what is happening in your life right now, but sometimes if we become more aware of our relationship with suffering and see that suffering comes and goes, we might have a different experience. Interestingly, we are more aware when joy comes and goes, than we are when suffering comes and goes. It's just a part of life. Thich Nhat Hanh, a Buddhist monk and teacher, once said, "The seed of suffering in you may be strong, but don't wait until you have no more suffering before allowing yourself to be happy. Even while you have pain in your heart, you can enjoy the many wonders of life—the beautiful sunset, the smile of a child, the many flowers and trees. To suffer is not enough."

Over the years, I have had so many clients tell me that if only one particular thing would happen in their lives, they could be stress-free and enjoy their lives. My client who needed to raise money to start her business told me that when the doors to her store opened her life would be set, and she would never complain again. A writer told me that he just needed to sell his screenplay, and he would be on his way and relieved. A parent told me she would be unhappy and stressed only until her child got into a good college. They all believed that if this one thing happened, they would have the key that opens the door to their peace and happiness. Yet, when the business owner was able to open her first store, she eventually started to suffer because she did not have enough money to open a second store. The writer sold his screenplay but, so far, the producers could not raise enough money to make the film. The woman's child went to a good college, but now she worries that her son won't find a good job when he graduates. So, each of them continues to wait for his or her key to unlock the door to happiness and success in the future when everything, fingers crossed, will finally work out.

As their suffering continued, life was passing. There was always an excuse for why whatever they had was not enough for them to find some joy and peace in the moment. Sometimes when clients come into my office, I name their suffering to show them the never-ending battle that they are waging against this moment. The business owner first had "I need money to open my store" suffering, and now she has "second store" suffering. The screenwriter had "I need to sell my screenplay" suffering, and now he has "making the movie" suffering. And the parent went from "my child needs to get into a good college" suffering to "my son needs a good job" suffering. I am sure that you reading this book can pause and think of your own type of suffering in this moment, whether it's how to solve a problem, better your career, or help your child, but you also may be ignoring what joys are in your life in this moment.

I am not minimizing any of my clients' suffering, but many of them kept exchanging one type of suffering for another when they might have been able to leave some space to feel other things as well. There are miracles unfolding in front of us all the time, but if they are not in line with our goals and stories of what we think needs to happen, we may miss them. It is so important to remember that even when we are struggling or disappointed, there are often things in the moment to be enjoyed and savored. Everything can become more important and sacred if we enjoy what we have accomplished, so bask in the sunrise and savor a cup of coffee or a conversation with a friend. It's not that all of your pain will disappear, but this mindset can bring a heightened awareness of the joy right in front of you to help you make the most of *this* moment.

One of the most important lessons I learned from my breast cancer scare is that suffering comes and goes. Joy comes and goes. Happiness comes and goes. Everything comes and goes. But the one sturdy thing that we each have within us is our choice about *how* we show up for every situation. *How* are we going to experience our suffering? *How* are we going to see our joy? If we choose to dig deep, be tender with ourselves, and be loving and kind no matter what shows up in our lives, we will be present, and we will be openhearted. When we do this, maybe we'll be more okay when the suffering comes, and maybe we'll be less attached to it. Maybe we'll find the joy in these moments and still find a way to live our best lives.

Try This Exercise: A New Relationship with Suffering

1. First, acknowledge your suffering. Understand that everyone suffers. Don't turn on yourself as if you are weak or can't handle what is happening. Acknowledge that everyone suffers and that there is nothing wrong with you for feeling the pain of stress, hurt, disappointment, or sadness about a situation.
2. Ask yourself what you are suffering from. Sometimes the suffering is from physical pain or emotional hurt. You may need to process it or use some of the tools from this book like maybe or acceptance.
3. Name your suffering. Do you have "career" suffering, "my child is doing poorly in school" suffering, or "I wish I could be happy with my spouse" suffering? When you name your suffering, it has less of a hold on you. It is as if, in naming it, you separate from your suffering on some level. How does that make you feel?
4. Think about the Thich Nhat Hanh quote, "The seed of suffering in you may be strong, but don't wait until you have no more suffering before allowing yourself to be happy. Even while you have pain in your heart, you can enjoy the many wonders of life—the beautiful sunset, the smile of a child,

the many flowers and trees. To suffer is not enough." What joys do you have in your life? Are you spending enough time with the people and things that you enjoy? Are you appreciating the people and things that you enjoy? How can the "many wonders of your life" share more of the stage with your suffering?

5. Sometimes there is suffering in your life that is significant, and none of these ideas alleviate any suffering right now. First, it is okay if these ideas don't work for you. Not every idea alleviates people's suffering. Stay with the feelings you are having and see if over time any of the tools in this book help you open the window and let some air into the room.

6. Last, female friendships can be very powerful and supportive when we are going through a tough time. Don't be afraid to reach out to the important people in your life. Most likely, your suffering is not unique, and they will understand more than you think.

Most importantly, remember that your suffering is not a sign of weakness but of strength and that you are not alone.

Chapter 7: February

Respond—Don't React: You Are *Not* Too Emotional

"Between stimulus and response there is a space.
In that space is our power to choose our response. In our
response lies our growth and our freedom."

—attributed to the work of Viktor Frankl

* * *

As I write this chapter, I am laughing. If I hadn't lived through this year, I am not sure I could believe everything that happened to me. In February, right around Valentine's Day, I was cleaning out the side table next to what had been my husband's side of the bed, and I found a Valentine's Day card that he never gave me. It read, "To My Darling Wife on Valentine's Day."

At first, it felt like someone was playing a trick on me, but there it was. I have no idea if he bought the Valentine's Day card last year and never gave it to me, or if it was one from long ago. The drawer was pretty messy. The drawer also contained the poem I wrote to him for his birthday the May before he left and the one he wrote to me for my birthday. I had shoved these in the drawer after he made his exit, and

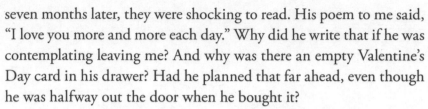

seven months later, they were shocking to read. His poem to me said, "I love you more and more each day." Why did he write that if he was contemplating leaving me? And why was there an empty Valentine's Day card in his drawer? Had he planned that far ahead, even though he was halfway out the door when he bought it?

I became consumed with anger. All I wanted to do was text him my worst thoughts. All the horrible things I thought about him as a man, as a husband, and as a parent. So much rage boiled up inside me that I felt like I had a temperature. As I grabbed my cell phone to launch one of the most epic spews of anger and hatred I would ever make in my life, I remembered one of my favorite quotes of all time: "Between stimulus and response there is a space. In that space is our power to choose our response. In our response lies our growth and our freedom." Immediately, on remembering these words, I was able to ask myself, "How will my actions serve me?"

I knew I was reacting, not responding. A reaction sometimes reflects our true feelings. But when we react, our emotions can come out in really bad ways. Other times, we are just reacting out of a bad habit, and our reaction doesn't reflect how we truly feel. Our reactions do not always serve us and often lead us in the wrong direction. Instead, when we are responsive, we take the time to understand how we feel, discover our actual needs, and find an appropriate action. When we take the time to be more responsive, we end up where we need to be.

This was the night when I started a practice of self-texting. In other words, texting my feelings and emotions to myself. I was trying so deeply to be responsive in every area of my life. I can't say that what I wrote was pretty or nice. I never knew that I was capable of that kind of rage and disdain, but there it was in blue and white on my phone. But that was the point. I sent it to *my* phone and not his phone. I don't even remember exactly what I texted myself that night, but I remember how angry I was and how good it felt to release it by writing it down and sending it to . . . me. I had always advised my clients to self-text, but now I was finally taking my own advice!

In the days to follow, if my husband asked me if I had paid a bill or how the children were or blamed me for the children not communicating with him, I would text myself, "You ruined my life. You should live the rest of your life in shame. How do you look in the mirror when you left your family? You are the biggest asshole I ever met." I self-texted even worse things that I will leave to your imagination. After I had some time to get it all out, and I calmed down, I was able to just respond to his questions: "Yes, I paid the bill," "I cannot control whether the children call you. I will let you know if there are any emergencies." There was no point in telling him about my rage because he didn't care, and it wasn't going to change a thing.

There is no shortcut to processing our feelings and emotions. Having feelings and emotions about events that life brings us is real and totally valid. I couldn't help being angry and disgusted with my husband that night and many nights after that. I wasn't *too emotional*, as women are too often accused of being, but I did have a choice as to how I would process my feelings and emotions, and that is a step that can lead women to more success and well-being. Self-texting was one of my biggest lifesavers! It allowed me to get everything off my chest, and over time, I was able to understand what I wanted to say to move my life forward.

* * *

For some reason, having "feelings" has often been frowned upon in the business world. When someone tells you to "act more professionally," they usually mean that you should keep a controlled demeanor and behave in a manner that is acceptable to the company. For women, this often translates into pretending to be okay in a culture that is not. In fact, how you pretend to feel is frequently more highly valued than how you actually feel. Sometimes "acting professional" can make us feel like robots.

The problem is that men created what we know as "corporate culture." They decided what behavior is acceptable, and women often have no choice but to follow along, or else get left behind. Corporate culture is what I call MFM: made for men. MFM culture rejects most of what society might deem "womanly" or—what they really mean—weak. So, very few emotions are allowed. And as I discussed earlier in this book, if a woman does display emotion, she is often perceived as "too unstable" for a job, a promotion, or inclusion in a critical discussion. Here is where it gets tricky: When a woman tries to fit into MFM culture, desperately trying to hide anything that might make her look weak, she's a "cold bitch." No matter how hard she tries, she is still a woman.

There is often no winning on the emotional spectrum for women because this corporate culture is just another way for certain men to perpetuate inequality in the workplace and remain in control of the economic and political power in this country and around the world. Many women blame themselves for their feelings, not fitting in, or not being more successful. Other women walk around holding on to anger because the glass ceiling is thick, dissatisfied that they can't get where they want to go professionally. When we walk around controlling ourselves from feeling, or blaming ourselves for our lack of opportunities, or just feeling stuck, it is tough to be our most creative, authentic, smart, and successful selves.

I've experienced this firsthand. I was on the board of my co-op building for several years. While on the board, I helped negotiate a thirty-million-dollar construction agreement. I was on the finance committee, and as a lawyer, I also dealt with most legal matters in the building. I never raised my voice in a meeting. I never cried or called anyone a name. I probably talked about certain issues like tenant matters in greater detail than certain men on the board would have liked, but that is more an issue of style and, for me, due diligence. Yet, toward the end of my tenure on the board, I found out that some of the men who held seats, too, thought I was "too emotional" and that it was hard to discuss certain things with me. In my experience, that is what men often say to try to dismiss a

woman's power when they disagree with her or when she is passion-
ate about or firm on a subject.

Furthermore, why should hiding our feelings or emotions be
considered professional? It creates stress and anxiety and makes us
sick when we hold on to what we want to express. I am not saying
you should go to your boss and tell him or her that you are suffering from anxiety because of how your coworkers treat you or how
much work you have, but as we explored in the last chapter, it is so
important to realize that everyone suffers. It takes courage to shed
tears and process your feelings. When you have strong feelings about
something that happens at work, it is for you to decide how you
want to handle the situation. I am not saying that you should cry in
front of everyone, but at least give yourself a break for how you feel.
It's okay to feel hurt when someone at work doesn't treat you well or
when you don't get a promotion. Yes, you can quickly accept the facts
of your situation to reduce some of your emotional turmoil and move
toward solving the problem, but you aren't too emotional if you have
strong feelings about the things that happen in your life. And you
don't need to act like an emotionless robot at work to succeed. If your
company's culture wants you to behave that way, maybe you need to
find a better place to work.

This is one of my favorite things about The Motherhood Center.
Here, there is a culture that supports the idea: *What you are feeling
is part of the job.* The women who work at the Center deal with a lot
of high-risk patients and the atmosphere is so supportive and collaborative. I have seen some women cry in a business meeting and
others express their stress or unhappiness with a coworker. I find that
when people are encouraged to express their feelings, work relationships are mended, people can release stress, and people can support
each other in the workplace. Better behaviors result from honesty
expressed with respect, good listening, and certain boundaries. It is
when emotions turn into destructive behavior that an organization
starts to have problems.

At the Center, we expect employees to express their feelings responsively, and when they do, we listen. I had a conflict with an employee at The Motherhood Center. We had worked on a few projects together, and some of our meetings felt tense and uncomfortable. I approached her, and we spoke about it. Certain behaviors of mine hurt her feelings, and there were ways that she dealt with things that I didn't like. We were both honest and didn't dispute what the other one was feeling. We acknowledged our conflict, recognized our mutual admiration for the work we both did at the Center, and found a better way to communicate so that we would have fewer misunderstandings going forward. This ended up being an easy conflict to solve because we genuinely liked each other, and we were simply miscommunicating. A lot of problems in the workplace do boil down to miscommunication.

Not every business conflict is as easy to resolve as my example, but it took commitment and responsiveness on both our parts to hear what the other person was feeling. And yes, there were also tears. But who cares? This woman is smart, dynamic, and amazing, and she had a moment with me. I honored her honesty, and it is a privilege to work with her at the Center. Once we cleared the air, it was an opening for ideas to flow again. In our meeting, we shared emotions, tears, frustration, respect, responsiveness, and openness to listen to the other, as well as a common goal to grow the Center. The result was a stronger relationship, better communication, and more collaboration.

I once heard a business consultant say that as a manager or boss, you should manage behaviors and not feelings and emotions. I understand what she was saying. In a way, you can't control how people will feel about a given situation, and in a business setting you can only monitor and try to encourage people to have "acceptable" or "successful" behaviors. But on a consistent basis, how people feel and what emotions they experience do lead to how they behave. Accepting people's emotions is part of creating an acceptable corporate culture that treats each worker with equality and empathy.

Feelings and emotions matter and cultivating responsive behaviors to express them leads to a better understanding of the needs of the employees and the organizations and what actions can be taken to satisfy both. In my experience, this shift in culture creates more employee work satisfaction, higher productivity, and growth.

One of the biggest challenges women face in our personal and business lives is how to be honest with our feelings and needs, while at the same time finding a way to express them in a manner that can be understood in the culture we work or live in. There is a good chance that we will be judged the minute we act outside the culture of an organization or relationship, which is why it is so important not to immediately react to a problem or concern and instead try to communicate these issues in a thoughtful, responsive manner. Can every problem in the workplace be solved if we are responsive versus reactive? No. But at least if you are responsive rather than reactive, your behavior becomes less of the focus, giving you a better chance of actually being heard. You might find the power to make a needed change in the company you are with. And if the situation doesn't change after you share your response to a problem, you might even leave and start your own business, go back to school, or get a new job that is better aligned with your mission and values.

Responsiveness can be challenging because it might feel less satisfying than the momentary satisfaction of telling someone off, but there is an art to how we communicate. Women are judged harshly in the workplace because of their emotional reactions, when in reality, men often react worse! I have never seen a woman throw something or punch someone at work, but I have dealt with several situations with men who tried to physically harm someone in the workplace and were not judged as harshly. I have known of fewer complaints against women than men for yelling or being condescending in the workplace. I have watched men have temper tantrums in the workplace far more often than women.

Furthermore, I have never seen another person significantly harmed by their coworker when someone expresses how a situation makes them feel or sheds a few tears or expresses their stress and worry. I am not saying that displays of emotion can't make a discussion difficult, but it should not feel threatening, disempowering, or degrading when someone expresses their own stress and worry. But when women show emotions, corporate America reacts as if emotions sink the ship, decrease profits, and make it impossible to work. So, by reacting less and being more responsive, it just removes the stigmas and deflections and possibly gives women a prominent voice at the table. And if your responsiveness, whether it includes emotions or not, is still dismissed or not listened to in the workplace, at least you did your best to communicate and you were collected enough to say how you truly felt about a situation.

***

While self-texting is a great way to ensure that your reaction to a given situation doesn't create unwanted consequences, if you have more time, when something happens to you or someone says something to you that you don't like, ask yourself, "How will my actions serve me?" This is the exact question I asked myself the day I found that Valentine's Day card. This question does not mean that every statement I make will end up serving me well, it just reminds me to look a little further down the road to where my reaction might lead. I found that when my clients and I asked ourselves this question, we became more responsive and forward thinking about the situation we were facing.

As I stated above, sometimes our initial reaction when we feel hurt is to want to hurt the other person back. We want to get revenge on that person, teach that person a lesson, or seek justice to make the situation right. But often, all that happens when we say or do something based on our initial reaction of pain or fear is that we create more pain and drama in our lives. We then have to deal with what that person said to us and manage the drama of how we reacted to them. Of course, we should stick up for ourselves immediately if we need to or if we think a strong reaction can move the needle on a particular issue. However, most of the time, our knee-jerk reactions force us to play defense instead of using our true power to be responsive and thoughtfully move our lives in a better direction.

Years ago, I had a client going through a nasty divorce with her husband. I spent most of my time trying to convince her that she should focus on moving her life forward at some point. (I never imagined that this situation would be a foreshadowing for my own life!) My client would gravitate toward action that would hurt her husband and give her satisfaction. That was her choice, and I don't judge it, but many of her actions were not in the service of moving her life forward.

When they still lived together but were in the process of separating, her husband would want to take the car to go out with his friends. But she insisted on taking the car each night. In the winter, she would often sit in the car a few blocks away from their house, freezing, just to spite him. She could have spent those evenings looking for a new job, seeing friends, doing yoga, or another type of self-care. Now more than ever, I understand that feeling of rage and anger. She wanted to hurt him. She blamed him and was trying to make him suffer because he made her suffer. I think the bigger question she needed to ask herself was, "How do my actions serve me?" Most of us would agree that she would have been better served only taking the car when she needed it and staying focused on moving forward. This doesn't mean we shouldn't fight for what we want or need, but just sitting in a cold car when your husband can just catch a ride from a friend—for example!—is not helpful in healing and creating a new life.

Once we've let our strong feelings out in a safe way that doesn't do us a disservice, we may see that we still need to respond. It is good to return to Viktor Frankl's quote: "Between stimulus and response there is a space. In that space is our power to choose our response. In our response lies our growth and our freedom." I find that the most successful women in business are the ones who can find a space between what has happened and their response. We should be honest with ourselves about how we feel so that we may assess our needs. When we can move from our reactions into our responses, we get better results. It is so tempting to react, but asking yourself, "How will my actions serve me?" usually leads to a more thoughtful response that goes a long way.

* * *

I am sure most of you can think of a person in the past few days whom you wish you had more kindness or patience toward during a situation or problem that arose at work. Maybe you wish you had reacted to a challenge at work differently in front of your coworkers, boss, or clients. You might wish you had been more thoughtful in your response. Or maybe an unexpected event caused a strong reaction internally and made you feel stressed or anxious for the rest of the day. We all have moments like these in our busy lives. Sometimes there is so much coming at us at once that it's hard not to react to anything that makes us feel like we are taken off course. When we find ourselves without time to self-text or ask ourselves questions, how do we gain more control over our reactions to our spouses, friends, bosses, coworkers, and children?

Most of the time, when I mention the Viktor Frankl quote to my New York City clientele, their initial reaction is, "I don't have time to do this." One client said to me, "I can't tell my boss just to wait five minutes before I respond to his question!" Another client said, "I can't tell my boss I need to go into the other room to meditate, or that I need to do some deep, loud breathing!" And another client scoffed, "Okay, I will tell my kids in the middle of their temper tantrums that I need to take a thirty-minute yoga break, and then I will be back." Although their responses are funny, each of these clients struggled because they felt they often did not say what they needed to in stressful situations. They sometimes became very emotional or stressed, which often affected their jobs, personal relationships, and health.

I would love for all of my clients to meditate twice a day and do yoga. I know from my own experience that these things help tremendously, but many of my clients claim they have no time. Also, even when we do these practices, many of us can still use extra help in softening our reactions to the world around us. The good news is that, even in our busy lives, there are still techniques that we can develop for ourselves to help us be more mindful.

To illustrate this, I would like to tell you a story about a time when I hurt my dominant hand. It was not a serious injury, but I tried not to use my hand for a few weeks so it could heal. Without the use of my hand, I needed to take things very slowly and think about each step in my day. Making a morning cup of tea, getting each item into my cart at the grocery store, and typing on the computer now took time and planning. I'm sure many people reading this book who've had a physical injury can relate to this experience. The most surprising aspect of this experience for me is that I was more mindful of my thoughts and actions in general because I was moving more slowly and focusing on the sensations in my hand. I started to react less to the situations around me and was instead able to have better responses to the world around me.

I noticed my softer reaction when my daughter left her winter coat and some wet towels on the bathroom floor and left the bathroom light on. Because of my constant awareness of my hand, I was more mindful of how I was moving and feeling when I entered the bathroom. I noticed a space between my feelings about her mess and my reaction. There was a pause that I did not plan. Normally, I would have approached my daughter with an annoyed tone. I might have raised my voice a bit, asking her to go back to the bathroom to clean up her mess and turn off the light. But that unintentional pause I took allowed me to be more thoughtful about my response. I immediately realized that it was not such a big deal, and I proceeded to think about how to turn off the light and pick up the coat and towels myself with one hand. I then calmly told my daughter not to leave her clothes on the bathroom floor and asked her reasonably not to do it again. The result? She did listen to me, and the next day she did not leave her dirty clothes on the bathroom floor. Instead, she left them in the bathroom sink!

After discovering the bathroom sink filled with her clothes, I entered the kitchen to find a sink filled with dirty dishes. I gently asked my other daughter to help me empty the dishwasher and load the dirty dishes from the sink. I had the space within me to make a choice not to get annoyed about the dirty dishes that had been left in the sink all day. The pause gave me a larger perspective and a greater appreciation for the bigger picture. I had not seen my daughter all day, and the pause allowed me to get through the dish issue quickly and enjoy the rest of the afternoon with her.

My injured hand showed me what mindfulness does for our lives. It also gave me a technique to use every day when life moves quickly. Focusing your awareness on a particular part of your body when dealing with a problem at work or home is a great technique. It leaves a part of you observing the situation from another point of view and brings a larger awareness beyond the situation you are facing. I fell upon this technique through an injury, and it has been a gift every day in my life.

Whatever technique you choose to use, greater mindfulness or responsiveness can allow you to show up for the unexpected events throughout your day with more emotional control and not let each event throw you off course. This leaves more room to cope with stress and worry and to find the calm and joyful moments each day brings.

* * *

The end of my marriage has been the most painful experience of my life. I have found myself having more intense reactions this year than ever before. I've felt everything in my life more intensely from extreme pain to extreme joy. I have cried more this year than I ever have in my life. I have spoken badly about another human being—my husband—more than I thought I was capable of. I have scraped the bottom of my emotions many times throughout the year. But at the same time, I have become a more responsive person. I have gained more insight into what I react to, what gets under my skin, what makes me feel bad or unlovable, and when I need to pause to assess how my actions serve me. I don't think my nervous system has completely healed from the shock of my husband leaving, but I understand myself better because I have taken the time to react less and respond more to everything around me.

Try This Exercise: Talk to the Hand and Text Yourself

We can use many techniques to create mindfulness so that we are less stressed and reactive to events and people in our lives. In response to my busy clientele, I created a simple exercise that you may want to try at your desk, when you are meeting with clients, or even when your boss is yelling at you.

1. Focus on one of your hands and become more aware of how it feels, what it touches, and how it moves for a few minutes. As you go about your daily chores or go to work, try to hold on to this awareness of the sensations in your hand. First, you may notice and appreciate all of the experiences you were not paying attention to before, from moving a piece of paper across your desk to how you hold the phone or a pen, how you type, eat lunch, or hug a friend. Even though you are doing different activities and your sole attention is not on your hand, the partial awareness that you draw to your hand will keep you more grounded and present. As your mind gets consumed with stressful thoughts at home or work, this is the moment when you are most in danger of overreacting to situations. Whether it is our children not listening, a disagreement with a coworker, or a difficult client, none of these things should overturn our apple carts. Our uncontrolled

reactions can damage our personal and business relationships and affect how we feel each day with a roller coaster of emotions. But by keeping a partial awareness of your hand, you will continuously bring some of the energy away from your mind and to your body, which will help slow everything down. You will become more mindful of each moment, and you may find that space between how you feel about a situation and how you want to react to it. This sacred space may help you show up with more ease, patience, and kindness for your children, spouse, friends, or business associates when you need it most.

You can also use this tool at the very moment when you feel your stress escalating. If you are getting very distracted with worry about the future or find yourself overreacting or feeling overly uptight, slowly bring some of your attention to your hand. You will bring mindfulness to your situation. And, yes, you can do this when your boss is upsetting you, and you don't need to leave the room for five minutes! You can do this during a child's temper tantrum, while sitting in traffic, or in any challenging situation.

I choose to focus on my hand, but whatever you choose, just find a place in the body to focus on. Your mind will calm down, and you will have a more centered response even if there is not a lot of time before you need to act.

2. Intellectually, most of us know that we should always "count to ten," but emotionally we can get overwhelmed with self-doubt, hurt feelings, bitterness, blame, or disappointment. As I said above, you are most likely not "too emotional." There is nothing wrong with these feelings and emotions, but if we sit with them too long or react too quickly, our thoughts and actions may lead us far from where we want our lives to be. Here are some questions to help you process feelings before you react in any personal or business situation so that you may respond in a way that will serve you: *Based on accepting*

my current situation, what do I really need to do to move for-
ward? Will my reaction invite drama into my life? How much
do I care about what was said? Does it change the value of my
life? Does this situation change where I am headed? Does what
happened change the things that are important to me?

After answering these questions, you will probably know
the response that will best serve you, so now you can ask,
"What is my plan?" Don't worry if you can't answer this
piece immediately but start to think about it. Ask yourself:
Do my current actions, conversations, or thoughts help me move
forward with my plan or what I believe is best for this moment
or the long term?

Only you can measure what's important to you. Only
you can decide if the momentary satisfaction of expressing
yourself in a certain way is what you want or if you prefer to
make statements that serve a long-term interest. You could
also choose to say nothing because you realize that you don't
really care about what happened, and you just want to move
on. And if you want to say something you know doesn't serve
you—self-text!

3. Even if things are moving quickly, a deep breath can also
   make a difference. A meditation practice, too, may give you
   the space you need without even asking these questions.

When you realize that space between a situation and your response
is the key to your freedom and success, you will find your own way
to let your unique voice be heard and share your special gifts with
the world in an atmosphere that respects who you are and what you
have to add.

You got this!

Don't Compare Yourself to Anyone Else

"The least of things with a meaning is worth more in life than the greatest of things without it."

—Carl Jung

* * *

I can't remember if my husband went to Cancun with "friends" in February or March, and I refuse to look at my credit card bills to find out. It is the mind's way of protecting you that certain things become a blur. However, I am quite sure that in March, my pain over that trip became an obsession. I took my younger daughter to Florida to see my parents, who are in their eighties. We hung out at their retirement community, and my younger daughter even saw her other grandparents, my husband's parents. So my vacation was about family, and his vacation was about volleyball on the beach with "friends." I felt abandoned all over again. I wouldn't even know how to go on a trip and leave my kids, who were really suffering. Who would they stay with? Who would I go with? I didn't even know he played volleyball. In the darkness of the night, I imagined who he was playing volleyball with (possibly someone on spring break?), which led me to a black hole of comparisons.

I have fallen into the pit of comparisons in the past, but it had been nothing like this. It was evident to me how damaging it would be to go down this road. I had also worked with several clients who became obsessed with ex-husbands or ex-boyfriends or girlfriends on social media. They were able to figure out who their exes were in new relationships with and became obsessed with their "replacements," too. I always had tremendous compassion for these clients but never imagined I would be at risk of going down the same road. I actually started to go on my husband's Facebook account to see if he had some new women on his "Friends" list, but after about five minutes, I just stopped myself. I realized I was in pain, but I was also reacting, and my reactions didn't serve me. So, I called a good friend, did some budget work for The Motherhood Center, and taped another podcast. It was clear that comparing myself to anyone my husband might be with did not move my life forward.

Someone told me once that comparing yourself to anyone is like comparing an apple to an orange. I always think about that comparison because it reminds me to ask, "What's the point?" I would never compare an apple and an orange. So, why would I compare myself to anyone my husband might choose to be with? It was just like trying to stop the rain. It was out of my control. I could make myself crazy or choose another direction.

Over the years, I'd had so many clients who were struggling with their exes because they believed that if their ex-partner was happy that they themselves couldn't be happy too. We forget that another person's happiness has nothing to do with our own. The world is large, opportunities abound, and possibilities are endless. If you just get off that Facebook or Instagram page, you will see that! We give our power away when we compare our lives to someone else's. It makes us believe that there is not enough happiness to go around.

Whomever our exes are in a relationship with are not the only people we compare ourselves to every day. I think many of us compare ourselves to people we work with, our friends, and even famous people we see in the movies and read about online. We might start to compare someone else's success to our success, how someone else looks to how we look, where someone else went to school to where we went school, how much money someone else has to how much money we have, and the list goes on and on. Whatever we're comparing, it usually doesn't make us feel good. And if it does make us feel good, the good feeling cannot be long-lasting because when we compare ourselves to others, we judge ourselves against a standard that's not authentic.

In my experience, when it comes to looks, women compare themselves more to other women than men compare themselves to other men. This is probably because women are more often compared to other women by the media, by men, and by society as a whole. In the workplace, I find that both men and women have the "comparison" problem, but it manifests differently when there is an issue in the workplace. In general, when men feel wronged and overlooked by a coworker or a boss, they often blame the company for being "stupid," "misguided," or "not knowing what they were missing." On the other hand, in a similar situation, I find that women are more likely to question their own abilities and whether they have what it takes to succeed where they are.

When women compare themselves too much in the workplace to their male and female coworkers, they can lose their voice and, quite frankly, lose their way. Yes, part of the success at work is understanding the work culture and what everyone else is doing in the company, but a woman's success in the workplace also has a lot to do with her ability to own her value, use her skill set to the best of her ability, and respect her power to speak up when needed. The phrase "compare and despair" is true! Women need to use their awareness and high emotional intelligence to look around their workplace to see if they need to improve their skills, but at the same time hold their power and know that they are capable, unique, and have value to add. If a company you work for refuses to see your value and treat you with respect and equality, it is not a place that deserves your efforts.

When I was in college, a friend of mine named Peter and I were both getting degrees in accounting. He was very ambitious, and he was always talking about his internships, job opportunities, and grades. I was feeling awful about myself at that point in my life. I had dropped out of an Ivy League university and was living at home with my parents, taking classes at a local university. I'm sure Peter didn't spend a minute comparing himself to me, but I constantly compared myself to him, and it made me feel even worse about myself. I felt like he had goals, and I didn't know what I was going to do next in my life. But I also felt like if he achieved his goals, there was no room for me to do the same. When we graduated, Peter got a job at a big accounting firm, and I went off to law school. I lost touch with him.

When I was in my last year of law school, I was walking through the main lobby one day, and I saw Peter standing there with a bunch of law books in his hands. Peter had ended up at my law school and was a first year. He had worked for two years as an accountant and then went back to school. There we were, years later, but in the same. exact place—I was even a little further along than Peter—and there was enough room for both of us.

The incident with Peter taught me a lot, yet when I graduated law school and started working in corporate America, I still didn't feel like there was enough room for me alongside my male colleagues. Again, I was challenged. The firm was a breeding ground for comparing myself to my male coworkers who were also attorneys at the firm. It felt horrible. There was something different about this than my situation with Peter at school, and when you look at statistics, it makes sense. The trend of more women going to college and being socially acceptable to pursue a career has been on the rise for a long time. In fact, from 1960 to 2000, the percentage of bachelor's degrees awarded to women increased from 38 percent to 55 percent.[13] Today,

13 National Center for Education Statistics (1995). Table 236, Earned degrees conferred by institutions of higher education, by level of degree and sex of student: 1869–70 to 2004–05. *Digest of Education Statistics.*

some studies suggest that total undergraduate enrollments stand at 57 percent women, 43 percent men.[14] Yet these statistics are not converting at the same rate to C-level executives, higher pay, and more funding for women's businesses.

Today, most women I speak to often tell me that they felt equal to men, for the most part, in college and during their graduate studies, although a majority felt that men dominated the social scene at most schools. Many of these women are quite surprised, though, about how marginalized, judged, and unequal they feel when they enter the workplace. For me, like many of the women I've spoken to, I was just as smart, creative, and ambitious as my male coworkers, but they were more accepted by the male partners at my old firm, and they got better assignments and more promotions. Very few women were "rainmakers," members of the firm perceived as bringing in money, because we had fewer clients and thus, no economic or political power at the firm. As I stated in an earlier chapter, no one was grooming me to make partner one day, not even the few women partners at the firm. It's not that I did not like my colleagues, but I felt that there was no future for me as a woman at the firm, and my comparisons to the men there made me feel disempowered.

All of this was so painful until I realized that the corporate culture did not align with my own values anyway. I didn't love the work (the legal tax consequences of claiming gas in a pipeline as inventory—seriously!), and the culture was harsh and cold. But it took me awhile to see that. At first, I tried to chase, please, conform, and do anything possible to "fit in" with the guys. I idolized the male power at the firm instead of realizing that I could achieve my goals on my own in a different way. It took many years and many male clients—I had my own law practice and then began business consulting and coaching—to finally stop feeling bad about not being treated like

14   Ginder, S. A., Kelly-Reid, J. E., & Mann, F. B. (2018). *Postsecondary Institutions and Cost of Attendance in 2017–18; Degrees and Other Awards Conferred: 2016–17; and 12-Month Enrollment: 2016–17: First Look (Provisional Data)*. National Center for Education Statistics, 6.

"one of the guys." I was never going to get the male acceptance I yearned for while being my authentic self. And this was true in other male-dominated realms, too. The men rarely asked me to go for beers on one of the boards I served on unless I asked where everyone was going. And that was okay, but I needed to find a way to stop feeling bad about myself. I needed to figure out how to harness my power and achieve what I wanted to in the business world.

Twenty-seven years later, men still have advantages over women in so many different industries. But even knowing this, there is no point in comparisons. The only reason we should look at what our male colleagues are doing in any industry is to determine how best to move forward. We cannot let our comparisons to any man make us feel less-than, incompetent, or hopeless enough to prevent us from achieving our goals. And there is no point in comparing yourself to the successful women you know either, except if you are looking for inspiration. Outside of these useful points of reference, comparison only knocks us down, and often prevents us from finding our way.

All of this does beg the question: If we compare ourselves to men in a way that might prevent us from achieving our goals in the workplace, what could we achieve by joining together to create a different company culture, and how can we do it? If this becomes our focus instead of dead-end comparisons, we may find an empowered or creative way to start shifting cultures at companies and move forward. Maybe there is another company where we can get a job and have more opportunities. Maybe we can start our own companies and create our own cultures where women can thrive, places like The Motherhood Center. Maybe we can even go back to school to pursue a career that truly reflects our goals and values.

The comparisons we make between ourselves and others can keep us locked in a company, a relationship, or a society that might not see us as equal. When we stop comparing, we can figure out our own truth, what we love, how we want to work, and what we want to achieve. Often, we are comparing ourselves to something that doesn't even represent us but instead represents what we *think* we should want and what we *think* we should be. But these belief systems usually rely on a culture that doesn't see women as equal, so we need to create a path that resonates with everything that we are.

Believe me, I get the challenges. I have seen men who have gone bankrupt, twice, raise money from other men more easily than a wickedly smart woman with a great business plan. I have seen women who raise money be sexually harassed by their investors or replaced by a male CEO who "understands" business better. I am not saying this is always the case because I have also seen fabulous male investors in women's businesses, but I find that men tend to invest more often with other men. In reality, women today do have opportunities for advancement in corporate America, but men have more. Women can get capital for a new business, but men can get it more easily—and they get more. Women can be on Wall Street, but men still dominate the financial sector. We find this across the board in so many industries. Yet, despite these barriers, we need to continue to forge our way.

As women, we need to be more innovative and creative to compete in the workplace, but that is just the reality. We have the ability to do it once we look within and stop comparing ourselves to other people, because the truth is, we don't need to be men to succeed, and we don't need to stay in corporate America to succeed if it doesn't work for us. I look forward to more women starting their own businesses in the years to come and becoming trailblazers and innovators for a new culture that is inclusive, diverse, and supports work-life balance for all.

Even if it is challenging and you must create your own opportunities, there is no point comparing and feeling bad about it. That is not where your power lies. Your power lies within no matter where you work and who you face. As the saying goes, "Where there is a will, there is a way."

* * *

So, what is one of the first steps? First, we have to stop comparing ourselves to men and to each other. How? Well, for one, social media can make us feel awful! I would be remiss in discussing comparisons without spending more time addressing the role of social media. It is so common to go on Instagram or Facebook and feel terrible when you get an inside look at other people's lives and think, *Why don't I have what they have*? It's not that you wish your friends and acquaintances ill but spending too much time looking at someone else's life can make you feel bad about your own.

Although our friends and family don't necessarily want us to feel bad when we look at their social media accounts, in a way social media is sometimes like watching an advertisement on television that makes us believe that if only we had what that person had, we would be happy and fulfilled. You don't even need to leave your house to feel bad about how you stack up against others. Now you can compare yourself to them without even getting out of bed!

I am sure most of you reading this book know that what people put on social media is just one moment of their lives and is not always a realistic view of their entire experience. We don't know the details of that moment they shared on Instagram or Facebook. We don't know what else is going on in someone's life. We might think to ourselves that everyone suffers, and the lives of the people we are envying could not possibly be that great. However, trying to make ourselves feel better by imagining other people's hardships is not helpful. It is not sustainable, and it also feels horrible after a while. Deep down, we really don't want our friends to suffer. We want them to be happy and fulfilled. It's just that we, too, want to be joyous and fulfilled.

Before I give you some help to embrace this new perspective, I want to reiterate how common the tendency to compare ourselves to others really is. I started to go down this route when my husband went on his Cancun adventure, but it happened on other occasions too. Last year, when I would go on social media and see some posts from a friend of mine, there was something about it that made me feel like I wasn't doing enough in my own life. She always posted pictures from her trips around the world, pictures of her at the best restaurants, art openings, book launches, and her success at work— and she always looked fabulous! Sometimes when I saw her Instagram account, I felt terrible that I had not done more with my life. I asked myself why my life did not look more like hers. But I caught myself and embraced the following perspective to get grounded and return to what I needed to do with my own life.

When we start to feel bad about our lives based on what some-one else has or is doing, we are just looking at what we don't have and aren't doing *in this moment.* To remedy this, we need to access a place of gratitude. With a gratitude practice, we are not saying we like everything that is happening in our lives, but instead, the prac-tice helps us find our inner and outer resources to handle what is in front of us. We all need a place to stand, and gratitude is always a great place to start. Ask yourself, "What do I have to be grateful for?" Sometimes we also forget the fullness in our lives because we are focusing on what we don't have. We can feel bad because we are trying to fit into someone else's life when we have a life of our own that is filled with many blessings.

And yes, this goes for how you feel about your coworkers or your boss as well. We must ground ourselves in our own blessings before we start looking at what we want to achieve. Sometimes we will find that our misery has nothing to really do with a coworker's life, and other times we might ground ourselves enough to see that there is an issue at work. Maybe this coworker gets better projects, maybe he has more friends at work than you do, or maybe he got the promo-tion and you didn't. But when you stop comparing yourself to this coworker and ground yourself in your blessings, you can use this coworker's outward success as a guide or lesson on how you want to move forward. Everyone has their own path, and if you are so busy looking at someone else's, you might just miss a few of your own roads along the way. While some of these situations might not be fair, if we use our wisdom from these experiences instead of feeling bad about ourselves because of what someone has achieved, we are more likely to stay empowered to fight for more equality in the workplace or create another way to be successful.

In truth, looking at someone else's life is like trying on a shoe that is not your size and expecting to be able to walk around and function. I actually sometimes think of that analogy, and it brings me right back to gratitude. I am thankful that I have my own shoes to walk in! It makes me laugh because it sounds kind of silly. But it does push me out of the thought about someone else's life and lands me back in looking at my own. So, the first thing you should do when you start to feel bad in relation to others is write down your blessings. It's an amazing place to start because it's so grounding to appreciate the life that we have. Acknowledging our blessings is the launch pad for removing ourselves from this downward spiral of honoring other people's lives more than our own.

Next, ask yourself what exactly it is about your friend's life, coworker's life, or whatever you saw on social media that is making you feel bad. Sometimes we just go into the spiral of feeling bad that we never ask ourselves why. What about the picture or post is making you feel negative? For me, after I did my gratitude practice, I asked myself this question regarding my friend's posts that had started to make me feel bad about my life, and I realized a lot had to do with my family not being together. I was also home a lot either working or with the kids, and I was missing attending more events and talks about spirituality. Although my situation was complicated, I signed up for a few classes and book talks with some friends, which definitely lifted my spirits.

When an advertisement or post makes us feel unworthy, unsuccessful, or alone, sometimes we need more than a quick fix like a night out with friends or some classes. I did enjoy those spiritual classes, but my friend's posts continued to highlight my hurt and loneliness. If you've ever felt this way, think of this as an opportunity to dig even deeper. Maybe it's okay that we feel this way. Maybe we need to recognize that we are feeling a lack in our lives and ask ourselves what would give our lives more meaning and purpose.

Someone once asked me when I was talking about this issue, "Well, what if I look within and find that I really want the success or riches or relationships that someone else has on Instagram, and I will never have it because it is not possible?" First, as I learned this year, no matter what is thrown our way, we need to try to make the best of it. We also truly have no idea what the future will bring or what is possible. The next step is embracing the unknown to start our journey. Maybe more is possible than we realize!

And as I discussed above, one of the best things we can do when we have these feelings is to look at our own lives and ask ourselves what will give our lives more meaning. This year, I have found that the search for meaning provides more stability, joy, and purpose. It offers direction and a reason to get out of bed. It doesn't matter what that meaning is, it just needs to be meaningful to you. Some people find meaning in their work, their relationships, in giving, or self-care—whatever it is, it just needs to be real for you. It needs to come from your inner self and not from a place that just looks good in the outside world. Meaning is long-lasting, satisfying, and brings a fullness to our lives that is sustainable. Thinking about these things today, I try to make choices and have experiences that are valuable, meaningful, and that help create the world I want to live in. Instead of comparing myself to my friend or getting trapped in feeling "lack," I use my feelings about her posts as a guiding light for staying on my own path.

Do your best not to make decisions based on what other people have, but instead on what gives your life true meaning. Ask yourself, "What am I not doing that would bring more meaning to my life?" If you're upset when you see someone happy on a vacation, ask yourself, "Would a trip be meaningful to me?" Find what is affordable, search for some great rates, and start saving your money. If you are on social media seeing all of your friends who are successful at work, ask yourself what you want to do, what would give your life meaning? It could have absolutely nothing to do with the job that your friend has, but it brings up something in you that is dissatisfied. Maybe you want more leisure time. Maybe you have a hobby. Or maybe seeing more of your friends and family would be meaningful. You can't let someone else paint the picture of what would give you a happy life.

I think we're all told we need certain things for a happy life, but whatever we think we need will only fulfill us if we truly connect to it. We can let these moments where we feel upset or jealous or envious be teaching moments, signals that we need to check back into our own lives and search for what is important to us. We might find that we already have what we need, or we might find that it is time for a change or that we just want to dig a little deeper into a certain aspect of our lives. Remember what Carl Jung said, "The least of things with a meaning is worth more in life than the greatest of things without it."

I had worked for a long time on not comparing myself to other people, but not comparing myself to someone my husband was playing volleyball with in Cancun was a new challenge. Still, the rules I lived by applied to this situation, and thinking about it was a waste of time. I am not saying that I didn't have intense feelings about it on and off, but after a while, I chose to focus more on me and where my life was going. I am still at the beginning of a new journey, so I am not sure what exactly I want for my life, but I do feel blessed for the life that I have, and I try to get to know myself and my desires better each day. I am sure that life will keep revealing my next steps to me over time. It is truly an expedition to get to know myself and to continue to look deep within. I don't think you will find me on a beach in Cancun playing volleyball. But perhaps Bali or the French Riviera . . . who knows?

Try This Exercise: Feel Good About Your Own Life!

Let's review the steps you can take when you start to feel bad about your life. This might happen when you are on social media, when you are at work, when you feel stuck, or when someone else seems to be moving ahead. You can also use this technique if you are watching TV or a commercial and seeing anything that makes you feel lack.

1. Remember the blessings in your own life. Write them down or make a mental list in your head. It is grounding to do this, and you might just find that you have so much joy in your life that you stop feeling bad about anything you were feeling inadequate about before.

2. If you still feel unhappy or bad or sense a lack in your life, ask yourself why you feel this way. Sometimes all that's needed is a quick fix like making a date with friends. Sometimes it is deeper. It is beneficial to use this as an opportunity to ask yourself what would give your life more meaning. The meaning can be simple, like seeing your family and friends more, or saving up for a great vacation, or making a bigger change in your life regarding work or a relationship.

3. If your feelings of inadequacy are about your job and you see other people moving ahead, ask yourself, "What does this person have that I want? Does that align with my goals? Does that align with my truth? How can I get that? How important is this to me? How can I achieve my goals and stay authentic and empowered?" You can want any life you want. It's okay to want. But when you compare yourself to other people, you may not have the energy remaining to manifest the life that you actually want.

4. Use maybe statements to stop making some of the comparisons that leave you feeling bad.

5. Use the apple and the orange analogy and realize that you can't really compare your life to anyone else's.

Remember, comparisons are a waste of time. You will be amazed at how much your life starts to change when you stop feeling bad about yourself because other people seem to have a more exciting or successful life. Instead, try to use the tendency to compare yourself to others only as a launchpad for creating more depth, purpose, and meaning in your own life.

Chapter 9: April
Maybe There Is Nothing Wrong with You

"Be yourself; everyone else is already taken."

—Oscar Wilde

* * *

SOMETHING about the winter had made me feel like it was okay to stay home and be sad on some days. But spring has a different energy. Spring invites you to smile and rejoice in the sunshine of life. The clear sunny days remind you that there is nowhere to hide. Winter felt protective, but spring revealed everything, myself included. With winter over, there was no excuse to stay inside with my daughter, watching her study, or hunkering down, creating more projections or budgets for The Motherhood Center. It's not that I never went out in the winter months, but my social schedule was in no way full. Now, I felt like I needed to leave the apartment and start doing something. Washington Square Park was the perfect antidote. It was exciting, full of interesting people doing interesting things, and would bring me some joy on the first beautiful spring day.

As I entered the park, it was filled with young NYU students, but it was also filled with young couples hugging and kissing. Even harder for me was watching all the young families. When my children were young, those days in the park were not always easy when they had temper tantrums or ran everywhere, including into the street. Sometimes it would amaze me that there could be a swing or a slide in front of my children, yet jumping into a loud city street where cars and horns were blowing always seemed to attract them more. But I had loved those days of young motherhood, and as I walked, remembering, tears streamed down my face.

I could not imagine a time in the future when my family would ever be together again laughing, strolling, and enjoying one of the first beautiful spring days. I wondered if I would go through the rest of my life seeing other families and feeling this way. And let's not even talk about the older couple holding hands and laughing by the fountain!

I knew I couldn't hide for the rest of my life in my apartment. I once had what all of those young families seemed to have that day in the park, but I didn't anymore. I needed to find a way to let spring in and let the sun shine on my heart again. It just felt so overwhelming to have a different life, a life I didn't plan for, and one that I, on many levels, still resisted. I had tried to stay very present throughout this year and not to project into the future, but at this moment I was overwhelmed with thoughts like, *How will I manage on my own for the rest of my life?* My suffering felt deep, and I wasn't sure I would be okay. I wondered again what was wrong with me that my husband had left me out of the blue. I felt so lost. I found a place to sit down on a bench by three men playing guitars and singing the Neil Young song "Sugar Mountain." It was one of my favorite songs when I was a teenager. As I sat and listened to the lyrics and the music, I began to relax. The song reminded me of a time before I met my husband, when I was single and had less pain in my heart. The sun was shining on my face, and it felt nice.

The sun calls you out in April to reveal what has been hidden. As I looked up toward the sky, I was reminded that I couldn't hide behind my husband anymore to be okay, and in truth, I was tired of hiding.

Many of us hide things about ourselves because, deep down, we do not feel okay. When we don't feel okay about ourselves, everything that happens in the outside world defines how we feel about ourselves in our inside world. The minute we are rejected by a potential partner or don't get that job, instead of seeing these things as experiences we are having, we start to believe that the external world defines who we are and that there is something wrong with us. And instead of working on our inner world, many of us hide what we don't like about ourselves or hide what we think the world around us would not approve of.

Not being ourselves hurts a lot and blocks us from truly living our best lives. Knowing that we are hiding something and believing that we need to in order for people to like us, to keep our job, or to get ahead—it can be so painful. The burden becomes greater and greater. We have no peace or rest and can't just be ourselves.

Sometimes we hide our physical insecurities by covering up a physical scar or dressing down because we don't want people to see our bodies. Sometimes we hide our emotional insecurities by being arrogant or not speaking up—in the end, these are opposite sides of the same coin. We often hide our true feelings because we don't want to feel vulnerable, we fear rejection, or we think we are not smart or capable enough. We often believe that if people don't see certain things about us, we'll be able to move forward and get the acceptance, validation, and success that we want.

You don't need nearly three decades in business to know that women hide themselves more than men professionally. I am sure most of you reading this book know this already. Quite frankly, many of us are taught to hide by our parents, our schools, our jobs, and the media. Men walk around with their stomachs hanging out, while many women get surgeries so they can "age gracefully." As I

discussed in a previous chapter, women are often seen as "too emotional" when they express themselves, so they often hide their emotions to succeed in the business world. Even when a man has to take
a bowel movement, he might strut around the office with a book as
he heads to the toilet, whereas a woman pretends she never makes
a bowel movement during work hours because it is not "ladylike."
And menopausal women are forced into hiding because they are less
desirable to men going through a midlife crisis. In my experience,
women are judged more harshly than men for practically everything,
so when we need to compete, find a relationship, make a friend, or
start a business, we often feel that being exactly who we are might
not fit the mold for success.

Consequently, most women are taught to hide parts of themselves to succeed in a culture that is not really rooting for them to be
the captains of industry, heads of hospitals and universities, or even
president of the United States. We are taught that if we act more like
men or if we achieve perfection, we can make it in a man's world.
Very few women I have met feel secure in all parts of themselves
or feel like they can go out and conquer the world. Many women
I know have a story of their parents supporting their brother more
when it came to business or education, boys getting more attention in
school, male coworkers having more opportunities, or men (like my
husband) leaving them to date other women. And one of the reasons
this cycle continues is that many women believe these limitations
and we hide pieces of ourselves just to get by or succeed.

When you hide, you don't really get to live your best life. You're
not willing to do certain things in your life because not showing
people your true self becomes more important. If we are buying into
a false narrative about who we need to be in our relationships or in
our work, we are supporting the status quo. In order to change the
status quo in this country, we cannot care what other people think
about us asserting our power. Because change is so difficult, when we
hold any part of ourselves back to compete with men who "let it all
hang out," we fail. Women need everything we embody, from our

emotions, quick wit, fearless ambition, kindness, and compassion to make those lasting changes that we want to see.

Many of us don't realize how much less we participate in our own lives when we hide things about ourselves. I have a friend who won't smile fully because her teeth are crooked. When she applied for a sales position through a headhunter, she got to the last round of interviews but ultimately didn't get the job. One of the criticisms that the employer relayed to the headhunter about my friend was that she didn't smile or laugh during the interview, which made the employer think that my friend might not have a pleasing demeanor. This is ironic because my friend has such a great personality. She told me that she didn't smile or laugh because she was covering up her crooked teeth. It was such a little thing, but any time we hide a piece of ourselves, our best selves can't totally shine through. When hiding out, you cannot possibly access all that is possible in your life.

Like my friend, many of us think that we are protecting ourselves by hiding, but all we are doing is hurting ourselves in the end. We have no idea which aspect of ourselves, fully expressed, may lead to our most extraordinary lives. We think we can work hard every day and hide our bodies, but this can inhibit us, whether at a work outing or while exploring new hobbies or sporting activities. We believe we can hide our emotions at work, but this can prevent us from moving our audience during a presentation or adding our uniqueness to a project to raise it to a higher level. We might feel distant from coworkers and not seem fully committed to the company we work for with our "robot" personality.

I can't even begin to count all the women I have met who told me that in order to succeed they haven't really been able to act like themselves. They have acted colder, less emotional, made fewer friends at work, and not always said what was on their mind just to get along. Now, of course, we can't say *everything* that is on the tip of our tongue all the time, but I am convinced that women trying to fit into a male-dominated culture or industry suppress so much creativity and innovation. I realize that there was a time when women felt "lucky" just to be in the room, but I argue today that we can do better. The problem is that the "standard" all women are compared to is a standard of how men behave in the workplace. Until women create a new standard, we will continue to hide our greatest instincts, creativity, and any assertion of our unfiltered power.

We all know when we're hiding. We put on extra makeup, cover up our bodies, or brag to compensate for what we are insecure about. We don't speak up at work so that we don't get anything wrong, or we hold back our opinions so that people will like us. We don't express our true feelings so that we are not hurt or disappointed. We don't pursue an occupation, start a business, or ask a guy out on a date because they might get to know the real us. Whatever part of yourself that you are hiding, see if you can create more freedom in your life for you to express who you really are to achieve your goals.

Dr. Catherine Birndorf's leadership at The Motherhood Center is a perfect example of what can happen when you don't hide. Dr. Birndorf is very comfortable with her looks and intelligence and is strong in so many ways. She is a force to be reckoned with. But I would argue that Dr. Birndorf never fully asserted her power in the workplace before The Motherhood Center. Don't get me wrong. She defended women's reproductive and mental health and was a renegade in her field, but she did it within a structure that didn't always reflect her own belief system. She strove for equality for women, but for many years she needed to be in a patriarchal hospital system to get her work done for her patients and in the service of women's reproductive and mental health. If you ask her, she will tell you that her mission was limited by the culture surrounding her in the hospital system, even though she always found a way to get things done and be well-liked and well-respected in her community.

What is so interesting about Dr. Birndorf's work at the Center is that she has created a matriarchy of sorts. I feel very proud to have developed a culture with Dr. Birndorf that reflects a supportive, productive, and profitable environment. We modify practitioners' work schedules to fit their lives, which can be tricky for the Center, but we make it work. The motto at the Center is, "If someone's life works, they will be better at work." Another policy at the Center is that feelings matter, but they can't turn into bad behavior. Which means, in effect, "It is okay to tell me you are stressed and I will try to help but don't take it out on me or anyone else." Dr. Birndorf believes strongly that everyone should be treated with respect and will not tolerate practitioners or other staff being humiliated in the office. Of course, a doctor still has authority when it comes to patient care, but everyone's voice is heard, and everyone feels valued.

I have never seen Dr. Birndorf put anyone down, and she is always curious and looking to expand her knowledge and grow. I have seen Dr. Birndorf compliment someone's shoes and then talk about raising $500,000 in financing and then help admit a very ill patient into the program. I think Dr. Birndorf is finding that the Center is a place that she can put all of her power and not hide anything about herself. She holds the mission of her business firmly and creates the culture she wants. I think she will continue to spread her work all over the country, if not the world, in the years to come. And, yes, she does have at least five different pairs of shoes in her office and changes them often.

Dr. Birndorf is a powerful example of a woman who is no longer hiding, but how can the rest of us get there? Believe it or not, it doesn't start with a medical or law degree or any degree for that matter. It begins with a healthy dose of self-love. In order to take the steps we need to live a fully authentic and powerful life, we first must accept that there is nothing wrong with us and that we have nothing to hide.

Create some awareness about what you may be trying to hide about yourself by asking yourself the following questions: What are you not letting someone else see about you? How is this limiting you? What are you not doing in your life because you believe you need to hide? How much pain is this causing you? How much freedom and joy would you feel if you believed that you didn't need to hide things about yourself from the world?

Now, try to recognize how hiding a piece of yourself from the world is like trying to hide from the air you breathe. It is like hiding from the sky. It is really impossible to do. It is an illusion you create. In reality, all that you are doing is limiting yourself. If you decide to stop hiding, you will experience all you can be from this day forward.

And when we are no longer willing to hide, it's like finding a place where we are comfortable saying, "This is me." We think that our flaws and other things that we are hiding will become impediments or disabilities when we let them out, but instead, they become great sources of light, strength, and resilience.

I am someone who has come a long way over the years (especially this past year!), but in the past, I used to let outside events play a big role in how I valued myself. The minute someone challenged me, I didn't always feel like I had the right or like I was strong enough to stand my ground and say what I wanted to say. Or if I did say it, I felt awful for days because I was so worried that people would not like me because I disagreed with them or if what I said was wrong. I had different ideas about solutions to problems than most of the people around me. Instead of valuing my ideas as unique contributions, I wondered, *Who am I to think differently than everyone else?*

I used to hide and compromise myself while volunteering at a not-for-profit organization years ago. Whenever I disagreed with a particular person on the committee, he would call me and say, "Allison, I'm really surprised. I didn't think you would think like that." Like clockwork, the minute he would say that (unless it was an issue that I felt extremely strong about), I would say, "Well, I don't really know if I think that. I'm not really sure." The truth is that when he challenged me, I didn't value myself enough to say, "Well, that's how I think, and I guess we disagree." A lot of us do that. I quieted my voice and hid my truth because I didn't love myself enough to be different.

When we don't genuinely love and value ourselves or when life does not go as planned, we feel horrible about ourselves. When our boss doesn't like us or we say the wrong thing, we feel horrible about ourselves. When we don't get a job or an opportunity passes us by, we feel horrible about ourselves. Again, we let the outside world control our inside world. It is not that these situations shouldn't make us feel upset or angry, and it is not that we can't still want things to be different than they are, but this is very different from seeing ourselves as *less*, as not deserving, as not valuable. When we allow disappointments to make us feel bad about who we are as people, every pain becomes deeper because we feel less than everyone else or less than who we really are.

So, how can we change this? How can we alleviate this pain of not feeling valuable so that we may stay on our path to achieve the things we want in life instead of hiding? The best we can do is find a way to make sure that we are completely committed to loving all of ourselves, not just the parts that seem "acceptable" to the outside world. We have to view our lives as a series of experiences that occur outside of our inner reality and how we value ourselves. We could like the experience, hate the experience, or want to change the experience, but the experience does not change the fact that we have a right to be here, voice our opinions, and love ourselves. We must create a strong identity that is separate from our outer experiences.

It is hard to start seeing ourselves differently than we have for most of our lives, and if you are like most women I know, you have struggled with self-esteem. Me being me, I started changing how I see myself with a maybe statement. The idea of maybe is gentle and undemanding and gives us another possibility, one that is different from the one causing us pain. I started to say to myself every day, "Maybe there's nothing wrong with me."

It might sound like a silly little statement, but the minute you question the ultimate doubt that you have about yourself, you give yourself the ability to reflect on your own worth. This simple statement allows us to contemplate the very real possibility that there is nothing wrong with us. With that possibility, we feel some of our wholeness. As we experience that feeling again and again, we start to choose the possibility more often that there is nothing wrong with us. The reason we do this is because it feels good to suffer less. We can choose to nourish our inner world that gives us the strength to handle the outer world with all of its twists and turns.

One of the first times I put this exercise into practice, I was in a room negotiating with eight men to sell one of my client's businesses. The men were a mix of attorneys and financiers. As soon as I walked into the room, I was thrown by who was there. I had no idea that there would be so many people representing the other side of the transaction. This was not a litigation where people were threatening each other, but it did get contentious at times. In my head, I must have thought, *Maybe there is nothing wrong with me,* at least once every five minutes. (Of course, I kept it to myself!) I sometimes laugh when I think about everyone around the table hearing my private thoughts as I was negotiating how much severance my client would get if the other side breached his employment agreement. But repeating this phrase in my mind stopped me from slipping and doubting myself. It stopped me from caring about how everyone in the room was seeing me. I knew I was representing my client well. It did not make me less aware of the nuances of how to negotiate. Instead, it kept me feeling whole, alert, and on point. I never doubted my value, so I was totally present for my client. I am not kidding you that by the end of the transaction, one of the lawyers said that if I ever wanted to join their firm, they would hire me. Obviously, I never took the job, but I felt great about myself, and my client benefited from those large severance payments many years later!

Think about it. How would you feel if the minute life stops going your way, you believe that there is nothing wrong with you? Again, this doesn't mean that you always say the right thing, act correctly, or that you should not try to do better next time. Regardless of what happens, you can still value yourself without going down the rabbit hole of thinking you are dumb or incapable or that no one loves you, and view whatever happens as an event outside of your value. The minute you don't feel like there's a hole inside of you or don't feel compromised, you will know what to say next, and you will know what to do next. Just as I was during those severance negotiations, you're going to be more solid on your path. That's just how it is. Sometimes this takes awhile to understand and accept, and you still compromise yourself, but at least at the end of the day you can go home asking yourself, "Maybe there is nothing wrong with me, and if there's nothing wrong with me, how do I really feel about the situation that happened today?" It sounds so simple, but it really works. It helps you get back to center and view your day more objectively.

This way of thinking changes your daily narrative. You start to realize that how you see your experiences is your choice. If we make a mistake at work or with a loved one, we made a mistake, but we're still just as valuable as we were yesterday. That's the thing—don't let the mistake make you feel less valuable. It is just a mistake. Could you feel bad about it? Sure. Should you reflect on what you need to do differently? Sure. Do you need to take responsibility? Sure. But it doesn't need to make you feel less valuable. Simply acknowledge that you made a mistake and try to do better the next time. This idea has changed my life. It has allowed me to go into practically any situation and feel whole even if I make a mistake or say the wrong thing. I don't spin out of control, and I stand my ground. If I have to apologize for something I did, I apologize. If I have to correct it, I correct it. But it doesn't make me less of a person. It doesn't make me less smart or less lovable.

The more you realize that there is nothing wrong with you, the more your authentic self comes out. And the more you are willing to speak up, the more inclined you will be to say how you feel, and the more your voice will be heard. You will start using your power to create new opportunities instead of tolerating less than you deserve.

It's funny. While you'll still experience conflict and problems, the more you see yourself as valuable, the more successful you will become, whatever success means to you. This is because you'll be out in the world, sharing your true beliefs and acting on your deepest intentions. This gives you the strength and resilience to stay on your path.

When you value yourself more, each situation becomes clearer. And it's okay if you want to change something about yourself. If you're not happy about your weight, you have a right to want to lose weight, but it doesn't change how valuable you are. You have a right to change your job. You have a right to have whatever experience you want to have. If you know that you are valuable all the time and if you are not thinking less of yourself, all of this feels so different.

I am very clear that the only way I am going to heal from my husband leaving me is to face the places I hide and completely love and value myself. If I let outside experiences dictate my value, I could easily write a story about how I am a washed-up middle-aged woman who will never be successful or fall in love because her husband left her to date more vibrant and successful women. But I don't feel this way at all. In fact, I love myself more today than I probably have my entire life. I had done all this spiritual work before my husband left, but I still hid the parts of myself that scared me or the parts about myself I didn't want to face. Since he left, I have stood in the darkness all alone and processed pain I didn't think I would live through.

But you know what I found? A really cool person who is lovable, kind, caring, super smart, and pretty funny when she doesn't take herself too seriously. I have a lot to say about business, and I don't need anyone's approval. And, yes, I've had losses, conflicts, and I have made bad decisions. But right now, my identity is intact because it comes from within. And if I can go from being one of the most insecure people I know to completely loving myself, so can you! Do I still have pain? Yes, lots of it. And so may you. But it hurts a lot less when I realize, maybe there is nothing wrong with me.

Try This Exercise: Be Your Whole Self

This is an exercise that allows us to remember our wholeness. It breaks the pattern of feeling less-than or putting ourselves down.

Whenever you feel like you're on shaky ground, raise to yourself the possibility: *Maybe there is nothing wrong with me.* When you walk around with this idea, the minute something happens in your life that makes you uncomfortable, unhappy, or upset, you are going to see the situation from the perspective of wholeness. This doesn't mean that you won't get upset or that there won't be conflict, but you won't be unraveling at that moment. You're going to see what is going on as an experience outside of yourself. You can ask yourself, "How do I feel? What do I want to do about this?" Separating what happens outside of yourself from who you are is one of the most grounding things you can do. It allows you to experience life with deep respect, trust, and value for your essence—and to share yourself with the world!

I hope you give these ideas a try because maybe there's nothing wrong with you. What a beautiful thought—to know that you were born with this wholeness. You were born with the ability to create meaningful experiences, achieve your goals, and find joy and peace in your life!

Chapter 10: May
Let Go and Let Life In

"Be happy in the moment. That's enough.
Each moment is all we need, not more."

—Mother Teresa

* * *

MY husband and I both have birthdays in May. We were born in the same year, eight days apart. I already mentioned the birthday poems we'd written to each other that I stumbled upon in February. As a perverse birthday gift to myself, I decided to read them again just to punish myself! Earlier in the month, I spoke to my husband for the first time since we separated. He sounded carefree and lighthearted on the phone while I cried for most of the conversation. He wanted to speak about money and let me know "he had a girlfriend." Learning that he had a girlfriend was like someone telling me one of my worst fears in life. But at the same time, I was quite aware that I was still breathing after he told me. He had been dating her for a few months, and I'd had no idea. I quickly asked myself, "What relevance does this information have for my new life?" I had immediate clarity that he and I were on the telephone talking business and that his girlfriend had nothing to do with it. It hurt, but it didn't knock me down. Little did I know that the knockdown was just around the corner.

We decided to separate a little money. We would refinance the apartment we both owned so that our two daughters and I could continue living there. We agreed to meet at the bank to open an account. I was so nervous to see him. As he sat next to me, I noticed that he had lost a lot of weight and changed the parting of his hair. He bought new fancy shoes and was wearing beads around his wrist. All I can say is that he would never have worn those beads on his wrist when we were together. I couldn't even imagine where they came from. After we signed the documents and he was about to leave, he asked me for a hug. It was one of the most jarring things I'd experienced since he told me he was leaving the previous June. For some reason, it was even worse than his telling me he had a girlfriend. It was clear that he had moved on, and I was like a platonic family member to him, someone to whom he offered a hug and some small talk. I did not hug him.

After I left the bank, I was outraged. I called Dr. Birndorf as I was reeling about what had happened. She was still talking me down and when I hit Forty-First Street and Sixth Avenue, I also hit the pavement. I was wearing high-heeled boots and tripped. It felt like I had been pushed down hard—by the universe.

As I lay there on the cement, I could feel my knee throbbing and my ankle in pain. What people don't realize about New York City is that people are incredibly nice when you need them. Three people gathered around me and lifted me up. I was so dazed that I am not sure I even thanked them. I limped in excruciating pain to the nearest Whole Foods, where I found a homeopathic remedy for bruising. My emotions were out of control. I got in the checkout line to pay, and I was sobbing uncontrollably, all the while clutching the bank documents that my husband and I had signed.

I was hardly aware of anyone around me, but I looked up and realized that standing right next to me in line was my twenty-seven-year-old cousin, Alexandra. Alexandra is loving and understanding and always gives the best hugs. She lives in Brooklyn and works ten blocks away from that Whole Foods. What are the chances that in the middle of New York City at two in the afternoon, she would be in the same checkout line as me? Alexandra hugged me as I sobbed. As she held me, it was as if everything in the universe was holding me together.

I immediately knew that it was time to stop telling and retelling the story of what had happened to me. My anger, my pain, and the story I was telling about my husband leaving me and the girls prevented me from appreciating what he had just done. He didn't need to sign the documents, and he didn't need to refinance the apartment, but he was trying to help out. I couldn't change the past, but I needed to recognize what had just happened in the moment. At the same time, I was being hugged by one of the most loving people I knew—my cousin. Funny, I did get a hug that day. Not from my husband, but from a person that I needed a hug from! I got the message loud and clear. Even when we are in pain, we need to recognize our blessings and have gratitude. But we can't see any of this if we refuse to put down what we are holding to enter each moment anew.

This moment reminded me of a story in Mark Nepo's book *The Book of Awakening*. Nepo tells a story about his friend Robert, who was determined to paint his family room. As he returned from the hardware store, he tried to open the door while carrying gallons of red paint, wooden mixing sticks, drop cloths, and some brushes. As he was trying to open the door and not wanting to put anything down, he lost his grip and fell backward on the ground, and red paint spilled all over him. Nepo writes about his friend's experience:

> Amazingly, we all do this, whether with groceries or paint or with the stories we feel determined to share. We do this with our love, with our sense of truth, even with our pain. It's such a simple thing, but in a moment of ego we refuse to put down what we carry in order to open the door. Time and time again, we are offered the chance to truly learn this: We

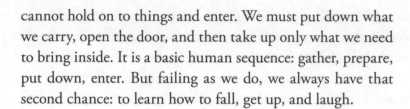

cannot hold on to things and enter. We must put down what we carry, open the door, and then take up only what we need to bring inside. It is a basic human sequence: gather, prepare, put down, enter. But failing as we do, we always have that second chance: to learn how to fall, get up, and laugh.

Since I read this in Nepo's book, I try to put down whatever I am worried or stressed about whenever I pass any doorway. I try to bring only what I need to the next moment. This has been extremely challenging this past year because there is pain I have not always been able to put down, but I tried to put down my worries about the future as much as I could. When I could do this, it helped me stay extremely present each moment and each day. I rarely thought beyond the day unless I had to put something on my calendar or prepare something for a later date. It allowed me to process all of my pain with less stress and worry and make the most of each moment, which enabled me to laugh and have joyous experiences even during difficult times.

I've also had a lot of success with clients over the years by sharing the idea of using each doorway as a symbol to put thoughts of stress and worry down before they enter the next moment. A great example is my client Charles from a few years ago. No matter where Charles was, he brought his office with him. If he was in the car with his children, he was on the phone doing business. If he was waiting for his child at soccer practice, he was on the phone doing business. He was always multitasking, even when his family was eating dinner. There wasn't any space for one thing because he was never putting anything down. He was so stressed and so worried, and he didn't have a lot of joy in his life. We worked on this for a long time.

For Charles, this idea of putting things down and entering into every moment new was really the thing that helped him the most. Just like me, he decided to use every doorway as a symbol to put down what he was holding to enter the moment anew.

Here is a description of one of his afternoons. The minute he left his house to pick up his children from school, he realized that he had passed through a doorway, so he would say to himself, "I'm going to put my work down. I'm going to put down that worry that I'm not going to meet that deadline for that client. I'm going to put down the fact that I have to get my taxes done. I'm going to put everything down because all I need to do right now is pick up my children." So, he made it a ritual to put all his thoughts and worries down when he left his house. He would take a deep breath, feel the sun on his face, and look at the beautiful flowers. When he opened the car door, it was another reminder for him to check in again. He would ask himself, "Do I have a clear mind right now?" When he got into the car, he would try to enjoy the music on the radio rather than have business calls. He was reminded of how much he loved to drive but had forgotten because his mind was always racing. But now, his mind was quieter, the radio was blasting, his window was open, and he felt the breeze on his face.

He began to see his children when he picked them up as if for the first time. His children got into the car, they all laughed and talked about school, and he gave them a snack. He then dropped one of his children at soccer practice and the other at a different activity. When he dropped them both off, he became aware that he had some work to do. So, he opened the car door to get back in, put his thoughts about his children down, and picked up his work again. It was the same routine when he picked up his children. When he got home, he picked up his work for an hour and then put it down when he left his home office and sat at the dinner table. He told me, "Dinner was thirty minutes of bliss. My children and my wife breathe oxygen into me. I love them all so much."

I know somebody reading the description of Charles's afternoon might think this sounds too simple, but it works. We don't realize how we accumulate everything that happens in every relationship and business transaction all day long and how it can affect us. We often don't put anything down. And it is not just about lessening our stress and having a clearer mind. We don't realize that if we get angry about being late for work or having an argument with our spouse or friend, we carry all of that into the next moment. Then, we might unnecessarily snap at a coworker or get extra stressed or anxious about a project at work because we did not start with a clear mind. Even minor things become a bigger deal when we don't put them down because we run the risk of ruining the next moment and carrying unhappiness throughout our entire day.

I have had the same type of success with this practice as Charles. I can have a problem I am trying to solve with a client, but then I have an appointment to go out for lunch with a friend. So, as I leave the door of my apartment, I put the problem down, which automatically creates space in my head. When I'm not thinking about it, I often find that an idea will pop into my head to help me with the client. The idea didn't come to me by concentrating on deep thoughts or feeling overly stressed. It came to me when I gave my mind space for something new to enter. The answers to our most complex problems are often singing to us if we are willing to make the space to listen. We do need to work hard to be successful, but without space within us, we never connect to all of our brilliance and to our highest creativity. It's almost like the space within us is the bridge to our greatness.

This is one of the most essential practices for a successful career, successful relationships, and just enjoying our lives. Life will always give us a reason to be stressed or blessed, and, yes, sometimes we feel both. Actually, I think if I was to sum up how I felt this year, that is exactly what I would say—"stressed and blessed." But as much as I could, every time I passed a doorway, I put down everything that was about the future, which allowed me to better experience the blessings in each moment.

When we can't put things down, we fail to recognize today's uniqueness even with its pain and problems. There are always moments to be experienced and lessons to be learned in every situation. Sometimes, when we can put our fears and worries down for just one moment, the detachment we create shows us what is important and gives us perspective. And even when we discover what remains crucial in our lives, we can still put down these things just for a breath, a hug, or a cup of coffee. We believe that there will always be another moment we'll have with everybody and everything, so we keep our minds occupied with work and our troubles, but that's just not true. Time passes, and life always changes. If we carry our stresses and worries to every single place because we fear what will be, we'll never get to enjoy our lives.

And that's why this simple practice is so important. It allows us to constantly empty ourselves as much as we can. What's so interesting is that the emptier we are as we enter each moment, the more we're allowing life to offer us new opportunities. If we allow the stress, mishaps, and arguments at work with our clients, coworkers, and bosses to accumulate internally, some of us will get anxious, sick, or overly burdened. We might become moody, lash out, and hold resentment toward the people we work with on a daily basis. Every time we see these people, we hold on to what they did last year, last week, and yesterday and it all accumulates in our mind. Our judgment of the current situation might be tainted. We might miss a great idea, an opportunity to collaborate, or a new possibility for success. I am not saying that we should accept people being rude, obnoxious, or discriminatory to us, but some upsets at work that we experience daily are small and meaningless. They don't affect our job or what we truly do every day, and usually we are just letting other people take us off our path, whether they mean to or not. When we are willing to put things down, we only pick up what we need for the moment.

If it's a big issue, you might not be able to put it down so easily, and that is fine. But often, most things upset us because other things in our lives are bothering us too. It is best to keep clearing our minds in each moment for each new situation. And as I discussed above, sometimes we can just put our stress down when we meet a friend for coffee or take a walk, and we can pick it up the minute we get back to our office. At least you can enjoy the cup of coffee and a short conversation, a pleasant stroll with some trees, or maybe, like Charles, you can put your work down for dinner when you get home and see your children for a bit before you need to pick it up again. Putting things down to enter the moment anew is about making better decisions with a clear mind, letting stress go for even just a moment, and getting the most out of the present so we can enjoy our life as it is happening.

The great saying, "No man ever steps in the same river twice, for it's not the same river and he's not the same man," really represents every moment of our lives because every moment is new if we let it be. Sometimes the most important question to think about each day is how can we let go? How can we let go of the hurt? How can we let go of the disappointment? How can we keep stepping into every moment of our lives, including every meeting, every business venture, every relationship with fresh eyes? We don't want to wait so long before we're able to make it right with the people we care about, and we don't want to delay living with less conflict. We don't want to wait until all the moments are gone to realize, "Oh, man. I wish I enjoyed that moment more. I wish I had been able to let go. I wish I hadn't been so stressed at work every day, because it really wasn't so bad. I wish I hadn't held so much against my coworker or my friend. Looking back, they weren't so bad."

Maybe you didn't get the bonus you wanted, or you weren't invited out with the "guys" at work or there are conflicts with coworkers. You still need to put down what you can as often as you can. Again, I am all for feeling your emotions, and if there is a real conflict that needs resolving, of course you need to protect yourself, but you will always pick up what you need. Just put down what is meaningless and not essential in each moment. This way, you enter each moment with more freedom.

Reach for gratitude and appreciation to see what really matters to you. And, yes, there will be certain things you're not ready to let go of, and there will be certain people you choose not to have relationships with anymore. But if you work on letting go, if you make a list of all that's important and what doesn't mean anything, you might find that each day feels lighter and that you have a fresh start with certain people. It's so beautiful when you see somebody and can look at them with fresh eyes as if for the first time. Creative and beautiful things happen.

This is exactly why I love this idea of doors because we're always coming and going. There is a door to our house, a door to our car, a door to our office, and a door to our bedroom. There are doors everywhere in our lives. If you make passing through a door the signal to remember what you need to put down in this moment and what you need to carry to the next, you're going to have more space and more presence in your life. You're going to have less stress. You're going to have less worry in your relationships because you're not going to hold on to things. Putting down burdens won't make you stay in relationships or jobs that are bad for you, and it might not speed up the process of when you are grieving or in pain. But it does remove the excess things that you don't need. It takes away what is petty and what you can let go of. It also allows you to put something down for a period of time, be it an hour or a few days, and then pick it back up when you need to face it.

For all women, this idea will help in the workplace and even at home. It will make us feel lighter and more joyous and will lead us to greater success. When you put down what you're carrying before entering a new space, you will be more creative at work and have more energy to get everything done each day because you will be carrying only what you need into the next moment. You may also find that, once you put them down, you won't feel the need to pick them back up again. Our road to equality in the workplace will not always be about fighting every wrong committed against us. Sometimes it will be about letting certain things go, learning our lessons, and becoming more empowered economically to create our own cultures and structures where men and women are equal. Believe me, I have spoken up a lot in my life when I have felt wronged or slighted, but sometimes I would have been better served to put down what I was carrying in the moment and just forge ahead. It is a delicate balance because there are wrongs in the workplace and in our society that must be addressed, but there are also times when we need to put down what we carry to enter the next moment as our most powerful selves. You will get the hang of it. You will know what you can put down and what you must carry. But you will also feel less burdened at times and more hopeful and energized to face each day, finding your path and empowering yourself in all aspects of your life.

This practice has been integral to my daily life since my husband left. Sometimes I could even put down all of my pain for an afternoon or a meeting, and other times I was only able to put down a minor hurt about a text my husband sent me. I had so many moments of bliss and pleasure when I could be truly present with an experience in front of me and, as the days are passing, I am able to experience even more freedom. I wish I could put all of my pain down right in this moment and open my door immediately to a new life. While life doesn't always work that way, I am gradually and slowly opening a new door. I hope that over time I will be able to put down the brushes, the wash clothes, and, most of all, the red paint that lives as a pain on my heart to find a new beginning. For now, I appreciate every moment in which I can lay the past down in some way. I appreciate every blessing that I experience. As I pass through each doorway, I think *Gather, prepare, put down, enter.* The days I can let go are the days I let in more new opportunities and possibilities.

Try This Exercise: Put It Down

As Mark Nepo said, "We must put down what we carry, open the door, and then take up only what we need to bring inside. It is a basic human sequence: gather, prepare, put down, enter." Keep that idea flowing in your mind: "Gather, prepare, put down, enter." It's a great mantra to use throughout each day to embrace all that is new in the moment before us. Use doorways to remind you. And when we fail to do so, "We always have that second chance: to learn how to fall, get up, and laugh."

Chapter *11*: June
Only Expect the Unexpected

"If you do not expect the unexpected you will not find it, for it is not to be reached by search or trail."

—Heraclitus

* * *

IT is June 30, 2019, as I write this, exactly one year since my husband told me he was leaving me. I am sitting in the same place I was sitting when he first told me. I started to get cold feet about finishing this book and sharing my personal story with the world. So, what did I do? I went on Facebook as I'd been doing every few weeks for quite a while to check his relationship status, and of course, today is the day I first notice—you can't make this stuff up!—that he removed his marital status, which in turn removed mine. Although Facebook doesn't announce when a relationship ends, it certainly notified anybody in my life that cared to look at my relationship status on my page. So instead of my announcing to the world that we were officially no longer a couple, he did it for me. I have taken it as a sign from the universe, or at least from him, that there is nothing stopping me from moving forward now but me.

I wanted to end this book with the story of how I have moved on, and how life is great, but things are messier than that. What I can say is that, in the twelfth month of my year without men, I am making sure that I learn my lessons. I don't want to get stuck in the version of the story of what happened that has me feeling wronged and in a permanent puddle on the floor. I had so many expectations for my life and my family. I wanted us to last forever as we started. But now, expectation is the place I can get stuck.

When life moves in another direction, our expectations can become a great source of pain. You can always find someone to support your pain and anguish over the life you expected to have, but this perspective makes it really hard for our lives to change. And often, the people who enjoy your story of pain are not so fun to be around.

There are definitely issues that keep coming up as my marriage continues to unravel, financial relationships shift, and my children struggle with the events that have taken place with both of their parents. But I don't want to dwell here. I feel as if I have told the story of the end of my marriage enough times. Whatever happens from this point on needs to be a story about me taking responsibility for my life, my choices, and my happiness.

I don't want to hang on to the anger that has been seething within me on and off during the year. Buddha said, "Holding on to anger is like grasping a hot coal with the intent of throwing it at someone else; you are the one who gets burned." These days, in order to let my anger go, I try to remember that most people are not all bad. Some people in my life would say that my husband is all bad, as if this idea can protect me and my children from pain, but it can't. And what's worse, there is something about this idea that keeps me stuck. It makes me feel as if I was deceived for the twenty-nine years that we were together. It makes me feel like I never knew him, and I never knew my life, like it was all a waste of time. A waste of a good life.

Whether I knew him or not, I try to focus on the good things in my life. I try to remember how he made me soup in the morning when I was on a strict macrobiotic diet. I try to remember how he took care of me when I had the flu. I try to remember family holidays and vacations. I try to remember that we brought two children into this world together. It doesn't lessen the blow of the disappointment and brokenness I feel from his leaving but knowing that he is not all bad and that our marriage was not all bad softens my heart a bit. I also realize that at this point, his happiness or misery gains me nothing. It doesn't change my journey.

In my experience, the place people get stuck the most after a bad breakup, divorce, or disagreement is in our expectations of who people should be or "should have been." These expectations, and the fact that they were not met, lead us to a narrow view that "people are all good or all bad." Whether it be our parents, our husband or wife, a boyfriend or girlfriend, or an employer, we want people to be a certain way to fulfill our needs, make our lives crystal clear, and most of all give our lives certainty. We want people to live up to our expectations of who we think they should be so that we feel safe within ourselves. When they meet our expectations, they are "good" people in our minds, and when they fail to meet our expectations, they are "bad." But often, the best things in life, the most successful ventures, and everything that is new and creative cannot be captured with clear lines and boundaries. Most relationships are not black and white. Most are messy and complicated, and at the same time, wonderful and interesting, teaching us how to grow and even love ourselves more.

Expectations are a story that we write about how we think our lives will move forward, what we think will happen next, who people should be, and how others should act. As you see from this book, I am all for having big dreams and goals, but when we expect something, it often steals from our present and our future.

One day in June, I had dinner with my parents who have been married for over fifty-five years. When I think about it, part of the reason I believed so deeply in the institution of marriage and the nuclear family was because of their continuous commitment to each other no matter the circumstances.

I never wanted my pain to cause me to miss a moment with my parents, so I have tried to make the best of my time with them this past year. I am fully aware that if I let my expectations of how I thought my life would be overwhelm me, they will steal away my moments of joy with my parents. I know that one day my opportunity to be with them will be gone, and this is an opportunity I don't want to miss.

I took my parents to one of my favorite Japanese restaurants toward the end of the month. I watched them walk into the restaurant as my mother held my father's arm. It was loud, and she had trouble hearing. She also expected the restaurant to be nicer. I watched my mother's expectations take her out of the moment. She wasn't enjoying the tea we were drinking, and she didn't enjoy the appetizers. She didn't like where we were sitting. And my dad, who was eating sushi (yes, I have an eighty-six-year-old dad that likes sushi), was comparing his meal to the sushi he usually gets in Florida. He was a little disappointed because it didn't meet his expectations.

Now, it's not that we had a bad time. We had a lovely time, but I saw these little expectations nibbling away at the overall experience for them, taking them out of the moment and creating dissatisfaction. And that's what expectations do in our lives—they create dissatisfaction. They allow us to create a narrative that things are not working out because they are not as they should be, and prevent us from seeing the wonder in each moment.

Interestingly, it had been about a year since my husband and I had sat at a Japanese restaurant with my parents and my sister's family. It was actually the weekend right after he'd told me he wanted to separate. I remember leaving my seat several times to go to the bathroom to cry. I couldn't eat, and I could barely speak. My family knew what was happening, but we all did our best throughout that meal to act normally although it was a bit awkward. The only one who didn't seem to struggle at all through the meal was my husband. Looking back, I think he felt so justified about how he felt so "right" that he had no remorse and just wanted someone to pass him the soy sauce and order more sake. He actually left the restaurant and commented, "That was an unexpectedly great meal," not even noting how I had hardly eaten anything.

Here I was almost a year later, sitting alone with my parents in a restaurant, not shedding a tear—and eating a sushi deluxe! This is surely not what I had expected a year prior, but now I wasn't thinking about any of that. I was just repeating the mantra, "This moment is enough," and feeling very present and blessed to be with them. I was quite aware that I might never have this moment again, and I wanted to squeeze every ounce of joy out of it.

So many of us don't see our lives as they are happening because we expect things to be a certain way. We think, "I'm always going to wake up in the morning, and my husband, wife, partner, boyfriend, or girlfriend is going to be there." We assume, "I'm going to eat this for breakfast. I'm going to drive to work. My job is always going to be there." It's as if we don't see the specialness of everything in our lives. But if you speak to people who have suffered significant losses, whether it is the death of loved ones, the loss of homes or other valuables, or the loss of jobs, they all feel the depth of what they lost. They often have certain regrets about not being more present, more mindful, and more appreciative of what they had when they had it.

Expectations can truly steal our happiness and joy, but if you're able to appreciate every moment, you're going to have a more joyful life. Simply waking up in the morning, moving your feet, and seeing the miracle of putting your feet on the ground is enough sometimes. So many things have to come together every day for us to have everything that we have. If we can cultivate an understanding of that preciousness, it changes the quality of our lives.

I had expectations for my life, my marriage, and my family. These expectations were so sacred to me that I based my identity on them and shaped my future around them. At this point, I believe that much of my pain comes from unmet expectations of who I thought my husband was, what we shared between us, and how I imagined our lifetime commitment toward each other. Family vacations, holidays, best friends, and coparenting two children all blew up on June 30, 2018. I can't change what happened, and I try every day to put the past to rest, but sometimes I feel like what stands between me and a new life is nothing more than an unmet expectation that I can't let go of.

Unmet expectations are filled with broken ideas. I've had clients who run businesses tell me that their businesses are not working. "I thought I would have $200,000 in profit this year, but I only have $50,000 in profit," they say. They thought they should have broken into this market or should have been able to develop one product or another that they didn't. The thought that their business is not working is just a broken idea of what they thought the business would or should be. To me, $50,000 in profit could indicate there is a blooming business that needs help growing sales, improving marketing, or opening new services or product lines. We uncover so much potential when we give up what we expected life to be. It creates more room to work today to achieve our dreams.

Expectations can also be tricky at work. In a perfect world, we would only work with people we love and only do work aligned with our deep truths and moral codes. But in business, we meet all types of people, and many are not ones we would choose to spend time with in our personal lives. Women often suffer the brunt of this because we don't always have the power to change the dynamic in the social structure of a corporation or culture in our society.

We can't always fire the client, leave the job immediately, or get reassigned, so sometimes we have to work with someone we don't like. What's often called for is a shift in perspective. To cope with our discomfort and protect ourselves, many of us paint people as all bad or all good. But the truth is, especially in the workplace, someone can be very moody or be so obnoxious one-on-one but extremely creative on a team. I am in no way saying that you should compromise yourself or subject yourself to abuse, but if you remain at a job, must maintain a relationship with a coworker, or need to keep a difficult client, you may get closer to where you want to be professionally if you try to hold a perspective that most people are not all bad or all good. Shifting away from expectations can help you see the reality of a situation more objectively.

We can also hold such deep expectations for our personal relationships about who we think someone is, or who they should be, that we miss the mark. I have stayed up so many nights wondering about the signs I missed in my marriage. How could I not have known my husband would leave? The truth is that we can only know people as much as they allow themselves to be known or as much as they know themselves. This means that people will always be different than we think they are, and if we get caught up in the expectation of who we think they should be, we will be very disappointed.

Often, we need to let people be exactly who they are and see if we can be okay with that. Of course, I am not talking about an abusive personal relationship—this must not be tolerated, and that behavior either needs to change, or you need to remove yourself from the situation. But most relationships in our lives are more complicated, so we must manage the ones we want to keep in a way that doesn't leave us feeling hurt or disappointed. Moving away from expectations will help us gain more presence and clarity. And the truth is that some of us get to a point where we no longer have a broken heart from the end of a marriage, partnership, or friendship. Instead, we are left with a broken idea of who we thought this person was, the relationship we thought we had, or what we thought would happen.

Sometimes I think about my parents' relationship, the relationship between my sister and brother-in-law, or my friend Robin's relationship with her husband, and it makes me cry. I will never have what they have in their lives—a long-term, committed relationship where they share everything, including their children. I am not saying that I won't have meaningful relationships moving forward, but I will never have that. I try not to get lost in the idea that what they have is better and that what I have is less. They just have something that I always considered to be sacred. But part of letting go of expectations is allowing everything to be as it is and not getting stuck in the broken idea of what we think our lives should be. Now, on most days, I expect the unexpected with open arms. If I want my life to change and evolve, it has to happen not in what is knowable within existing expectations, but in the vast and wonderful unknown!

Try This Exercise: Expect Less and Get More!

How can we stop our expectations from stealing the moment? How can we stop our expectations from blocking the miracles in our lives? How can we stop our expectations from creating a distorted view of what our life really looks like today?

1. The first thing we can do is to be aware. We need to try to enter each moment with an openness. Every time I go to a restaurant, try something new, or go to work, I try to be open and curious and not expect my meal or my day to be a certain way. It's not that I will eat a meal at a restaurant that tastes bad because I committed to having no expectations. I'm still going to honor my likes and dislikes, but it's important to try not to fixate on things having to be a certain way. Sometimes the restaurant could look a little shabby, but the meal could be great. Other times, the meal is awful, but the company is wonderful. But because you didn't have any major expectations, what goes wrong is not such a big deal and what goes right feels like a sacred moment. This invites you to go with the flow more and see how life unfolds.

2. We must work on shedding this idea that everything in our life will always be there. I don't bring this up to upset anyone, but I do so that you can understand the miracle of everything you have in your life. The miracle of a friend, the miracle of food, a job, a car, a tree in front of your home. Whatever it is, expectations cause us to take our lives for granted. When we drop this idea that we expect everything to always be there, we see the wonder of everything around us. It's probably one

of the most poignant, beautiful, and fulfilling things you could do in your life.

3. We must also try to separate which feelings and pains are real from the ones that are just broken ideas. If you don't get a job that you thought you were going to get, it doesn't mean anything is broken. You just had an expectation that this was *the job*, but most likely, there's still a wonderful job waiting for you somewhere. You just have to keep moving forward. Sometimes we have a relationship, and it ends. We can get so stuck on the life that we thought we would have had together, the family we would have had, and the lifelong commitment we believed in so dearly (believe me, I get this one!). When it's over, yes there is heartache, but after some time it becomes a broken idea, and you will have a hard time moving through it and past it if you're not willing to let it go. As I am learning the hard way, after a period of time, the more we keep talking about what "should have happened" and "how it was supposed to be," the more our unmet expectations will block new things from coming into our lives—new hope, new possibilities, new opportunities, and new love.

4. Play around with the idea that most people are not all good or all bad. I am in no way saying that you should stay in an abusive work environment, tolerate less, or compromise yourself. But there are times when we shut down so quickly because we don't like how a coworker or boss acts at work, but we choose to keep working at the company because there are a lot of other great things happening. If we can step back and see how everybody and everything is usually multidimensional, we might see some of the good in a person or situation, which might help us move forward with our own career and success. This one is a little tricky, but if you love and trust yourself, you can handle the nuance of this idea and use it to achieve more in your life!

Sometimes we're living our best lives, but we fail to see that behind our expectations or fears we might not be okay. But life doesn't have to happen the way you thought it would happen for you to be okay. There are so many ways to be okay. There are so many paths by which our lives can move forward if we're open enough to follow them. When you drop your expectations, you find your strength, you find your resilience, and you live with an open heart that will always lead you to your best life.

Chapter 12
Build the House
You Want to Live In

"If you feel lost, disappointed, hesitant, or weak, return to yourself,
to who you are, here and now. When you get there, you will
discover yourself, like a lotus flower in full bloom, even in a
muddy pond, beautiful and strong."

—Masaru Emoto

* * *

FOR me, it is a new year. I am hosting my podcast, working at The
Motherhood Center, and I even took on my first male client in over
twelve months! It did feel a little strange at first to leave the circles
of women I'd been in, but I love helping people and, ultimately, suffering is gender-neutral. My children are adapting to their new lives,
and I continue to process my pain and try to begin a new life as what
I believe is a more authentic me.

As I look all around me, women are making their voices heard
more in court, politics, and on the world stage. More and more are
making it to the C-suite. Although women appear to be making
some headway in our quest for more equality in the workplace, there

still exist very strong societal structures that dictate how successful we can be in the world if we don't conform. Some of you reading this book might be totally liberated from these constructs, while others are totally stuck. But the barriers that some of us are experiencing hold all of us back. We need to knock old constructs down and build new structures based on our authentic needs and desires for our lives.

The business world was built for men and by men, so true equality might never be achieved by women within the constructs that currently exist. In my perfect world, more women will start new businesses and new workplace cultures based on principles that breed real equality for everyone. While corporate America is alive and well and not always supportive of women as equals in the workplace on many different fronts, I believe that it can evolve as women keep cultivating and asserting our power in society.

Regardless of the landscape around us, we must find a wholeness from within to have the strength, resilience, insight, and innovation to create new structures that support our evolution. I believe that the lessons from this book will help women do just that.

I just got a call from a friend who tutors high school students for the SAT. My daughter is about to start studying for this test, so she said to me, "Make sure your daughter doesn't get bullied by the test." Her point was that she wanted my daughter to be more self-assured in her thought process and answers so that she doesn't start doubting herself too much when she takes the test. I asked my friend if in her twenty-year career she found that more girls get "bullied" by the test than boys. She laughed and said, "Absolutely, a girl is more likely to blame herself for not knowing an answer, and a boy is more likely to blame the test!" She then said, "I've had boys blame the answer key for being wrong before they blame themselves!" We both laughed, but there is a real truth to what she said.

As the mother of a sixteen-year-old and twenty-year-old, I've witnessed my young girls and their friends be so much more doubtful than their male peers, and I know that this can carry over as they get older into the workplace. As a society, I think we marginalize women from a very young age, and many enter the workforce already expert self-doubters. Then, their environment frequently does not support them to grow, but instead reinforces their lack of equality, insecurities, and any doubts they may have faced as children and teens.

Again, this is why I share my lessons learned from my year without men—so that you can transcend these norms and reenter your work and home lives feeling fully empowered and equal from within. Only when we do this can we make empowered decisions that will actually impact the outer landscape of the business world to achieve true equality and, most of all, freedom for all.

As a last thought, I think it is essential to look at the following three questions to frame all of these lessons I've shared and to understand how we can all move forward: What relationships do you need to be joyful? What job or occupation do you need to be successful? And who do you need to be to find joy and success?

The first question: What relationships do you need to be joyful?

When I was in my late twenties, I'd look around and see a group of women in their sixties walking down the block. As I passed them, I thought, *All these poor women don't have husbands*, or, *How sad that their husbands couldn't be with them tonight*. I'd see two young girls on the street without a guy, and I would think, *How sad that they don't have dates tonight*. I know it sounds crazy. The people that know me well always saw me as a liberated woman (after reading this book you know better), but I was brought up to think that you need to have a relationship with a man to make life meaningful and happy. I always believed that women should work for a living, be independent, and speak their minds, but I was still attached to the construct about having a relationship with a man, thinking it would lead me to a happy life. I believed that whoever didn't have this type of relationship should strive to get it. I didn't judge single people, but I'm now ashamed to admit that deep down, I believed that something was missing in their lives, and I hoped that they would find it.

It is clear to me today that this construct about needing a man is sold to us to separate us from our true economic, social, and political independence. A bunch of women in their sixties walking together down a block could be just as happy—if not happier—without any men, and two girls walking outside on a night out? Well, maybe it doesn't get better than that. I'm sure many women did not buy into this construct when they were in their twenties, and there are likely even more today who don't believe it, but I didn't know that this construct had been sold to me. I didn't know there was another way.

I have spent this year looking for peace and trying not to regret any decisions I've made with relationships in my life. I now know that I was sold a narrative of what my life needed to look like, and I never continuously evaluated deeper questions, which I try to do every day moving forward. I know people who have no partners and are very content living alone. I know people who are divorced and live very fulfilling lives. I know people with relationships in their lives of all different kinds and embrace the joy that it brings them. It's a vast undertaking to allow ourselves to figure out the life that we want to build for ourselves because it might exist outside the "norm," but how can we know what we need in our lives without first asking what brings us joy and what structures in our lives no longer work for us? Without asking ourselves these questions, we get trapped with what society tells us is right or best.

Now to the second question: What job or occupation do you need to be successful?

Ask yourself, "What's going to make me joyful?" You might choose to make a lot of money and not care that much about what you need to do (of course, legally!) to earn it. That's fine. You just want to create your own structure for your life and not live in the constructs created for you by other people. When we're looking to choose a career, people might tell us to go to a particular school for this occupation or pick this job. "Go to law school or become a doctor, and you will make a lot of money," we'll hear. But there are many other jobs and occupations you can do that might align more with your passions and creativity. And yes, it's great to be an attorney or doctor if you love it. But the narratives around where you can make money and where you can't, which is the safest path, and "what you should want for your life" steer us into certain jobs until many of us we wake up one day in our thirties, forties, fifties, or sixties asking ourselves, "What did I do with my life?" Many of us feel financially obligated to support our spouses, kids, friends, or communities, but looking more in-depth at our true desires leads us to more creative, expansive, and fulfilling lives. This allows us to take care of ourselves, and often those around us, even better.

I've repeatedly seen people pursue more authentic lives to create the abundance they both need and desire. It takes hard work and determination, but so much more is possible when we live with an open heart and mind. Some of my most successful clients over the years have started businesses that seemed outlandish at the time. Yes, some failed, but others created new industries, and one of them just sold their business for hundreds of millions of dollars!

The last and most important question you need to ask yourself is: Who do you need to be to find joy and success?

My hope is that this book helps you figure this question out. You don't need everything that our society and culture say you do to find joy and success. We must look beyond these walls, these houses that were built for us, and look deep within to find what will make us whole—and not apologize for it. Some people will look to societal norms for these answers. They need the job. They need the husband or wife. But those of us who are willing to look beyond and acknowledge our truth—"I'm in pain because I'm not living an authentic life"; "I'm in pain because I'm staying at a job I don't like"; "I'm judging other people's lives because I'm not satisfied with my own"; "I'm accepting less in my relationships"; "I'm not speaking up"; or "I don't like the rules that I've been taught I need to follow to succeed"— have a chance to find ourselves and be free.

Building a new structure for your life doesn't mean that you need to reject or hate men. There are many wonderful men out there, a lot of beautiful marriages, and many different types of relationships between different genders. This book is about finding yourself beyond the world you may have been taught to accept and showing up as your authentic self to achieve equality, find fulfillment, and accomplish your mission on your own terms.

We need to look at all of these ideas and decide which parts of our lives we are willing to accept and which ones need to go. For me, this journey happened during a year without men. While my greatest construct was taken from me in a very abrupt and painful way, my hope is that you will choose to do the work to make necessary changes in your life with greater ease, intention, and grace.

Maybe I would never have fully embraced myself had my husband not left me and had my work life not conspired to surround me only with women. I certainly would not have seen all the things women give up in the business world to get along and survive instead of succeeding and thriving. I am not sure if things in life are always meant to be, but I do believe that we need to make the best of whatever life gives us, and that comes with being responsible for our lives, learning our lessons, and loving ourselves unconditionally.

I didn't see all of the places I hid my power or accepted less for myself. I have worked hard this past year to create a new foundation in my life. I am building on this new foundation with strength and resilience to help me stay on solid ground. Looking back on this year, even through the pain, suffering, and anguish, I love myself more, accept myself more, and trust myself more. My heart is open, and I am compassionate toward the suffering that everyone feels at some point in their lives. But the biggest lesson might just be that there are *so many different ways to be okay.* And when life takes an unexpected turn, I still believe that life is full of possibilities.

It's been a year. How do I feel? Hopeful. For myself. For my girls. For women. And for our world which, because we are women, we are working to make better every day.

Acknowledgments

FIRST, I would like to thank my wonderful agent Leslie Stoker. I remember sitting across from you at the Marlton Hotel when you said those magic words, "Okay, let's do this!" and here we are. Thank you for your insight, kindness, and brilliance. I also would like to thank Kyra Ryan for helping me edit the many versions of this book. Your magic with words, understanding of my work, and friendship are so meaningful to me.

With deep appreciation, I want to thank my publisher, Skyhorse Publishing, and my editor Nicole Mele for getting behind this project and supporting my vision. I also want to thank Sara Sgarlat, my longtime publicist and friend. Your support for my work over the years has enabled me to reach so many people and inspires me to continue on my journey.

I would not have made it through this year without some beautiful women in my life. My mother, Lorraine Naiztat, and my sister, Diane Naiztat, were anchors for me throughout this year when I was trying to navigate a situation that felt impossible at times. My deepest love and appreciation for my dear friend Robin Miller, who devoted hours each day listening to me cry, making me laugh, and holding me. I would also like to thank the many women who gathered around me for even just a few hours but ones who held my heart and made me feel like I could carry on. There were so many, but I would like to say a special thanks to: Kate Walbert, Mary Lynn Nicholas, Merrill Rudin, Libby Johnson, Elizabeth Cuthrell, Wendy

Ettinger, Jamie Levitt, Lynn Harman, Hari Kaur, Griff Fairbairn, Anna Backer, Madeline Vaz, Marci Zaroff, Astrid Marzovilla, Kim Holden, Devorah Meadwin, Naomi Naiztat, Debbie Kaye, Mara Kaye, Alexandra Kaye, Erica Naiztat, Anna Valencia, Sarah Edwards, Melinda Cheng, Rachel Lloyd, and Stepanie DiLibero.

I would like to thank my teacher, Cathy Towle, and Reiki soul sisters Sholmete Yoo and Sonya Shoptaugh. Becoming Reiki masters together and exploring the spirit of the universe in the middle of New York City was oxygen and transforming. A special thanks to Maria Soledad, a spiritual guide and a beauty queen who lightened the way from the first minute my heart broke to the woman I am today. Your support was truly inspiring and lifesaving. I would also like to thank Barbara Wosinski, a wonderful human being and healer, for her guidance and love during a very challenging year.

Alexandra Max, who started me on my spiritual quest many years ago, I miss you very much and pray your soul is at peace.

A special thanks to Dr. Catherine Birndorf, one of the most incredible women I have ever known. Thank you for your support, love, and trust. I would also like to thank all of the beautiful women at The Motherhood Center with a special thanks to Paige Bellenbaum, Donna Klassen, Lisette Gali, Sharon Axelrod, and Elizabeth Baron for many special and loving conversations that helped me get through the day.

I want to acknowledge Dr. Meredith Lash, Dr. Barbara Edelstein, and Dr. Elisa Port for their dedication to women's health and the kindness and compassion they showed me.

My dear friend and Women4Women Summits partner, Joan Herrmann, you are an angel who was sent into my life. Thank you for all of your support and kindness throughout the year.

My biggest thanks and deepest appreciation go to both of my strong and resilient daughters, Morgan and Amanda. None of us expected to go on this journey and I am so proud of everything about who the both of you are.

And to all of you who have read this book. My sincere wish is that this book gives you some strength and hope that you have what it takes to go out into the world with your unique gifts and succeed—it is more than possible! Sending much love to all of you on your life's journey.